Sick & Twisted
in Savannah

Sick & Twisted in Savannah

Memoirs of the Victory Street Irregulars

Sadie Allran Broome

gatekeeper press

Columbus, Ohio

Sick & Twisted in Savannah: Memoirs of the Victory Street Irregulars

Published by Gatekeeper Press
2167 Stringtown Rd, Suite 109
Columbus, OH 43123-2989
www.GatekeeperPress.com

The cover design was created by Mary King Patel. She is a graphic artist living in Washington Island, Wisconsin.

ISBN (paperback): 9781662900228
eISBN: 9781662900235
Library of Congress Control Number: 2020937169

Contents

—◆—

Acknowledgments

———◆———

This work of fiction could not have been written without the patience of my husband Dennis and the encouragement and editing of my daughter Stephanie.

The inspiration for the work was my five great friends, Susan, Diane, Jo Anne, Phyllis, and Sharon. It is a treasure to find lifelong friends! They, along with Julie and Teresa, were excellent editors as well. All of these poor souls have heard and read these stories so many times!!!!!!! Bless.

Introduction

—————◆—————

Back in the 1980s, an inner-city school in Savannah, Georgia had a number of vacancies. Six teachers were hired from various spots around the country. These teachers found themselves in a stressful situation. They were in culture shock, had to make new friends, and were far away from home. They went on to have numerous adventures with humorous, lewd shenanigans. This is their story.

Murder House

———◆———

This is a memoir of my time teaching in inner-city Savannah, Georgia. I met five teacher friends and we bonded over many adventures while getting to know our school culture at Victory Street School. We forged a fabulous friendship and had wonderful, spirited adventures in a great city. This is just the first part of my crazy life in the '80s. Prior to the start of my story, I had been serving a life sentence in the home of my youth, Cherryville, NC. Cherryville is a friendly town of about three thousand people. I was paroled from Cherryville when my daughter and I moved to Macon, Georgia so that my husband, Paul, could attend law school. Tina Dawn is my daughter from a former marriage, but Paul and I married when she was three so he has always been there for her.

Leaving Cherryville was easy. NOT!! I had never abandoned Cherryville to live anywhere else. I cried the first six months. My family's Christmas gift that year was that I finally adjusted to Macon and stopped crying.

I won't talk anymore about my three years in Macon right now. I only mention it so that I can tell you something else.

After my husband graduated from Walter F. George School of Law, our course was set for Savannah, Georgia for Paul's first job as a real attorney. You see, Savannah is where this story really begins.

I've heard that when Georgia was established as the 13th colony in the 1700s, Savannah had only 3 laws: no slaves, no liquor, and no lawyers! We wanted to fit right in, so we began our stay with Paul violating one of the sage old rules.

Disclaimer: *Before I go further, you must understand something about this narrative. My story is made up of things I have seen, heard, implied, or made up. Often flat-out rumor may become a fact of my narrative. I cannot say this strongly enough: I am not researching anything for this story. The previous statement about Savannah's 3 laws is just something I've heard. If you want to know if it's true, try the Internet. It is kinda like my narrative, part fact, part rumor, and part total fabrication and you can never be sure which is which.*

Our new Savannah home was off Victory Boulevard on Paulsen Avenue. When you think of the beautiful old South, picture this Boulevard crammed with live oaks and beautiful old houses. Our home was a duplex that fit right into this style of old southern charm. We were in one half of a large duplex with a fireplace, a Florida Room, a screen porch, a detached garage, and a nice grassy yard. The rent was inexpensive. We could not believe our good fortune that such a nice place in such a wonderful neighborhood was available.

With my husband at work and our daughter still in Cherryville for the summer, it was up to me to begin setting our house in order.

While unpacking, the power meter guy came and asked if I was scared to live here. Thinking of nothing better to say, I asked, "Why?" He told me that there had been a murder committed right in this house. He said that HIS wife would NEVER want to live in this murder house. Later, the nice man from the phone company showed up and we had a similar conversation. I began to feel some bad karma building up. I felt a shiver and a bit of the wee willies. Oh! That's bull. I was scared shitless.

It was time to talk to the only other person whose phone number I had in Savannah, my husband. Yes, his law firm knew all about the murder and the attendant rumors. It seems that it had inconvenienced the firm since the young lady victim was a court reporter who was scheduled to record a deposition for the firm on the day of her death.

Apparently, she was found in the bathtub in MY HOME stabbed multiple times in the chest. Some think her beau was the culprit. The boyfriend lived in the other duplex. You see, the two apartments were connected by the attic. (You could go into my attic and look down into the other apartment.) No one was ever convicted of the crime. The needle on my "creepy meter" was pinned at the max.

I decided to take a break and get a little positive karma goin'. I decided I needed to know someone in town other than my husband, so I went to the house next door to meet the neighbors.

My next-door neighbor answered the door and I introduced myself as Annie Bell, her new neighbor. Apparently her well of human kindness was empty that day. She replied, "We keep to ourselves and hope you will too!" She went on to tell me that her husband was a former police officer assigned to the murder case in my home and that he has always maintained that the victim's best girlfriend committed the murder rather than her beau. He said that the number of stab wounds was consistent with a female perpetrator.

I went home to continue unpacking and to try to make sense of the strange past that belonged to my house. Since I am a teacher of children with emotional disabilities, I had observed that bad girls are more dangerous than bad boys. Girls tend to 'overkill.' That murder seemed to have the mark of a woman all over it.

Day one: my neighbor hates me and we live in a murder house. This sucks!!

Even though we lived in a "murder house," we accepted our situation and moved on. Paul and I enjoyed exploring Savannah. Paul had done an internship in a Savannah law firm the summer prior, so we had some friends already. One of our friends was Buck, Paul's neighbor. They lived in, what was called at the time, a "transitional neighborhood."

Paul liked the old historic house. It was an old Victorian house that had been converted into apartments. It had a turret with a clawfoot bathtub. It was so cool to take bubble baths with windows all around to look out and see Savannah. Lewd and lascivious activities could happen in the tub and no one would know!

We spent a lot of time with Buck and wanted him to meet a girl. We introduced him to Lois, who was the sister of Paul's law school buddy, Sue. Buck declared that he would never marry a redhead, and of course Lois was a redhead and he did marry her. Buck also was a master gardener with a special talent for growing the plant known as Cannabis, Mary Jane, marijuana – his plants were very healthy. Buck came home one day to find his whole crop clipped away. No plants for Buck and friends. Another day that same summer, Buck came home to his apartment, and as soon as he entered the house, it was apparent that he had been robbed. The perpetrators stole his clothes and his gun. Buck saw the robbers and chased them. That was how he realized they must have stolen his gun, because one of them shot at him right out there in broad daylight, in the hood, with *his* gun!

Savannah was America's first "planned city" and it was designed in shady squares. Many of the squares have historical monuments. The riverfront section of Savannah is historical, beautiful, and charming. It is often known as the sister city to Charleston, South Carolina. The Savannah River runs through this southern, genteel city. In the early history of Savannah, many merchants conducted business getting items from the ships that came in. That area became known as "Factor's Walk." There is a riverfront walk with shops and restaurants and the streets are cobblestone. It is a quaint tourist area, but fun for the locals as well.

There was a bar we would frequent named Kevin Berry's Pub. Kevin Berry's, of course, is an Irish pub. A large population of Irish immigrants settled in Savannah.

A popular drink that Paul and I both enjoyed was the black and tan. It is Harp and Guinness beers in layers. This takes skill for the bartender. They use a spoon as the beer pours to create the layers. The wait staff got to know Paul and I. Often when we were there singing along with the Irish band, the waitress would come up to Paul and say, "Oh my, someone ordered this who did not want it, would you like it?" Since I had only part-time summer jobs, a free beer hit the spot.

Spanky's was a tourist-friendly restaurant on River Street with very good food. Local law enforcement cops maintained a presence on River Street to keep the peace because they want happy tourists who come back to their city. One of the officers was usually standing outside Spanky's with a chicken finger basket that he would offer us as we passed by. We always stopped to converse with him. He would always just happen to not be hungry.

Paul did not always love the street sales on River Street on Saturdays. That is because it was hard for me to not spend money. There were crafts and unique items every week. I bought the neatest leather sweater one Saturday as we were strolling down the cobbled streets. Yes, I did say "leather" sweater. Even though we had limited funds, there was shopping to be done.

Dawn, Paul's sister, and her husband Jimmy came for the weekend. I brought Buffy, my second mama. Back in the day, in the South, people had maids. She cooked, cleaned the house, and looked after me and my brother. Buffy would be called a nanny today. She gave me soul and spirit. It was only natural that she would be invited to Savannah; she helped raise me, and she had a huge hunger for the opposite sex. While we were all walking by Spanky's, the next thing we knew she had her arms around our favorite policeman and we had to literally drag her away.

We had very little room in Paul's apartment. We slept on pallets on the floor. We all loved that bathtub in the turret. Jimmy tried to tell Dawn to be careful in there, but we all heard her squealing as she sat back in the clawfoot tub and the water ran out on the floor like a tidal wave.

Of course, we ended the weekend with more shopping on River Street.

Horses, a Shark, and a Kiss

———— ◆ ————

I have already mentioned some of those weekends the summer that Paul lived and did an internship in Savannah and I was in Macon, Georgia doing various summer jobs. This particular story happened during that crazy summer.

Ruth, my former special education teacher's assistant when I taught in North Carolina who became a reading specialist, was still a BFF. I still kept in touch after our move to Macon. I knew that she would enjoy coming to visit on a Savannah weekend. We both have had beach vacations together before, and just like Lucy and Ethel, we always have a crazy kind of fun.

Ruth was coming to Savannah, and Paul and I were so excited to see her. When she got there, we did the usual and took her to the tourist places on River Street. We went to Spanky's and Kevin Berry's for drinks. Then we went to eat and drink Hurricane Punch at the Pirate's House.

I remembered that Ruth and I had often talked about how we both liked horses and had ridden in the past.

I am no equestrian, but I do have a love for horses. Things have never seemed to go the way I plan when horses are involved.

Just thinking of horses reminds me of one of the stories from my misspent youth. One of my first boyfriends, who turned out to be my cousin (is that a Southern thing or what?), and I went with my long-time girlfriend Jean and her boyfriend at the time to go horseback riding. We were riding toward Cherryville proper when a big storm came. Those horses went crazy! They started running through people's yards. We had to duck to keep from getting clotheslined. We got to my house on Elm Street to park the horses until the storm ended. Then we were able to ride the horses back.

That night, Dear Cousin called. He had written a song about us called "Side-Saddled Annie, What a Fanny." Isn't that the most romantic thing you have ever heard????? (Actually, my fanny is one of my outstanding assets.) If you don't think that says romance, that is OK. I was about 13 at the time. I really did not know then that having a romance with your cousin might be a bad thing and could produce some strange children with a family tree that does not branch.

My dad was less than impressed when he spanked me to get me out of bed and shouted "get up right now, you have work to do in the front yard" as he handed me a shovel. You have not lived until you have shoveled horse shit out of the front yard in Cherryville proper in your pjs.

Now that that remembrance is over, let's go back to my tale with Ruth. In Savannah, I had heard of a place that you could go trail-riding for ten dollars. I thought this would be great for Ruth and me, so we went out to the stables and paid for our ride. They brought the horses out and helped us on. We were so excited and began to lope away from the barn. Of course, I thought my horse was the prettiest, until he turned around and tried to bite me. "I don't know about this Ruth."

As soon as those damn horses got out of sight of the barn, they galloped away. We could not begin to control them and were careening through people's yards in a nice neighborhood and out on the street. Ruth and I were cussing and hanging on to our horses for dear life. I guess if you could put a good spin on this nightmare, it would be that at least the horses stayed together. When they finally got tired and headed back to the barn, the owner came out, not very pleased with our performance. He said that if we ever came back there, we had to ride the goats. Honest to God, believe it or not, the next time I saw Ruth she said that she wanted to buy a horse. Me, not so much.

Poor Paul was working as usual, so Ruth and I went out for an adventure on Tybee Island, a barrier island near Savannah. The island is the easternmost point in Georgia. The famous phrase, "From Rabun Gap to Tybee Light," contrasts a mountain pass near the state's northernmost point with the coastal island's famous lighthouse (taken from Tybee Island website). I wanted Ruth to get to see this unusual beach. We had previously traveled together to Myrtle Beach, SC – a wide beach with nice brown sand. The beach there is quite populated, with high rises and restaurants and bars everywhere you look. Tybee

Island was not very populated and had no high rises in the '80s.

Tybee Island is a barrier island in Chatham County, Georgia, near Savannah in the southeastern United States. The name Tybee Island is also used for the city located on part of this island.

It had just rained and the air was crisp and wonderful. We were able to wander down the beach and pick up shells that had washed in from the storm. I loved elegantly shabby Tybee Beach!!! The sand is not white; it is like gray clay. The water also is not Caribbean blue. It is a shade of gray, but the sky was blue. We would take a break every now and then and go back to our chairs, towels, and cooler and sip a bit on our fruity and grainy PJ's. That would always elicit stories and giggles and gossip about our mutual friends and our past teaching adventures in North Carolina. Those conversations would usually have the words, "bless her heart" or just "bless."

One story we loved to tell was about the time that we left a centerfold from "Playgirl" magazine on the copier, and the principal made an announcement on the PA system. "Someone has left something on the copy machine they should come get right now." That was a "bless our hearts." This was the same principal who walked by as my sixth-grade student, Robert, was helping me take down a Christmas bulletin board. I was standing on a chair and was wearing this cute, long Christmas plaid pleated skirt, knee-high socks, a red sweater, and a bow in my long brown hair. This outfit was way too much of a temptation for this particular principal, who came up and whipped out a Polaroid camera, flipped up my skirt, and took a picture. He thought that would be SO funny, until he realized that *I wore no panties.* He ran. We laughed about how scandalous that was for years to come. When I applied for my job in Macon, he gave me the picture to put on my resume. The other funny thing is that the last day of school that year, my student Robert kissed me on the lips as he was leaving for summer. I guess that was an experience that he will never forget either.

As we wandered on another beach walk, we found something very unusual. It was a shark that had washed in. Yes, really, seriously. Usually you only get the big old jaw of teeth, but this shark still had the cartilage attached. We thought it was exceedingly cool. You could see the big jaw full of teeth; its body was slimy and gray. It was so big that both of us had to carry it in. We were humming the theme from Jaws we were so excited. We could not wait to get this amazing find home to Paul. We gathered our stuff and made two trips, one for our stuff and one just for Mr. Shark. We put him in the back of my Mazda and made the journey to Paul's apartment. We carried the shark up to the top of the stairs and stretched him across the doormat and threshold to the apartment and yelled for Paul. "Honey, Honey, Honey, you won't believe what we found out on Tybee Beach."

Paul came to the door and had such a look on his face. It was not the face of admiration or awe that Ruth and I anticipated. "Oh my God, what is that horrible smell? That may be the worst odor of my life. That is *not* coming into our apartment. Tomorrow, Jaws must return to his natural habitat, the beach!"

Ruth and I were disappointed. Over martinis, we regaled Paul with stories of the beach and our fabulous day. I was sad that we had to say our goodbyes to Ruth the next day, but I think Paul was a little relieved to have some sanity restored to his life. Soon, I would travel back to Macon to work and he would have a few days of peace.

Time for Annie Mae to take old Mr. Shark back to Tybee Island. Bo, the parking lot attendant, came up to my car window and said, "What is that smell?" He actually called the Savannah police because the shark smelled like a dead body. The police arrived rather quickly and verified that it was not a human. Imagine that. They were *super* sharp.

About the same time, the beach lifeguard appeared for duty. He came up and heard about (and smelled) my odiferous shark. The amazingly handsome, blonde, and buff lifeguard said that we should drive my shark out to the museum. He said they might be interested in it since it was an unusual and very fresh specimen. We carried the shark and put it in the back of his, thankfully open-air, Jeep Wrangler. As we were getting in the car, he asked if I would like a breakfast drink of can shake. That is like the PJ that Ruth and I drank on the beach. Good old grain alcohol and fruit. That just says breakfast to me, so of course I said yes to the offer.

When we got to the museum, they were glad to get this unusual find. My shark turned out to be a lemon shark. I was ecstatic. We got back in the Wrangler and the lifeguard turned to me and said, "Do you realize that you readily got into a car with a strange man and even accepted alcohol? Let me just say that you did not know my intentions and you don't know them now." I began to sweat. Then he advised me to never do that again and asked if he could have a kiss. Seriously. I was in my thirties and he was considerably younger... But did I not earlier say blonde and buff???? Of course, I had my kiss and then we headed back to the beach. What a totally fabulous day!!!! My shark made it into the museum and my lifeguard was not a serial killer and was a good kisser to boot.

Wrong Place, Wrong Time

———— ✦ ————

I was a little depressed when Ruth left. We had so much fun. Now, Paul was at work, the shark was in the museum, and I was facing a long afternoon by myself. I get bored easily and decided I should be a good wife and do Paul's laundry before heading back to Macon.

Paul had told me specifically not to go to the laundromat alone since we were in a "transitional neighborhood." Of course, I listen *so* well. I put the laundry in a big basket and headed straight to the "do not go to" laundromat.

I don't know about you, but 'laundromat' is almost like a dirty word. A word as dirty as his dirty laundry. You have to haul all your stuff away from home and have a purse full of coins and sit and be yet again bored while you wash, dry, and fold. You are using industrial washers and dryers that have been used by hundreds of people washing their dirty laundry. I was never good at following directions and have trouble figuring out how to operate the machines, and then I am also lazy about laundry and mix the colors and whites, which as you know is a big no-no. Pink underwear is not Paul's favorite choice. I was going to be in trouble today no matter what!

Well, I got the laundry into the washer. Then I noticed some teenage boys loitering. I was not sure why they were there. It did not appear that they were doing laundry. As usual, with my keen powers of observation, in no relation to Sherlock Holmes, I paid little attention to them. I washed, dried, and folded my clothes. I was thinking that this misery was almost over and I would get to eat an early dinner with Paul. It was then, when I least expected it, that the boys ran over and stole my purse! They ran out the door and I ran right out after them chasing them down the street. I was yelling, "Stop you little bastards!" Of course, that worked – not so much. They ran faster and dropped my purse. I was pissed, but I did go retrieve my purse. At least all they got was $10 and my red sunglasses. That was all my money. Too bad for the little bastards. I was planning to use my $10 the next weekend to go back and ride my horse again. Well, that was not such a good idea anyway. Maybe I was better off. I went back and got my laundry and prepared to be pitiful as Paul gave me a good "dressing down" because as he says, "I never listen."

Why was I looking forward to dinner? We had no money. Paul's dinner choices consisted of Vidalia onion sandwiches, chicken livers, or leftovers from Krystal's that I had brought with me for the weekend. Paul surprised me and said that we had enough money to head out to Tybee and eat at the Sugar Shack. I loved that place. It had a whole list of burgers to choose from, and the cheeseburger is my favorite food. They even had a 'cannibal' burger that was raw. We rode out to Tybee on Paul's motorcycle. It was a great way to finish such an exciting and eventful weekend.

Orientation, Meet the Irregulars

---•---

The Irregulars' story takes place in the mid-1980s at Victory Street Elementary, which was built in 1929 as a community school for African-American students. An impressive three-story, red-brick building, the school was integrated in 1979 with an unusual plan: middle-class fifth and sixth graders would be bused to Victory Street from the suburbs, while kindergartners would draw from the low-income neighborhood. The building had not been updated with air conditioning (what, make education funding a priority?!), so the numerous 90-degree temperature days would be challenging.

I was looking forward to getting started. One of our first activities was an orientation for teachers new to Chatham County. The central office invited us out for a riverboat cruise down the Savannah River. It was a gorgeous riverboat with a large paddle wheel on the front set to cruise through the historic riverfront. It was a sunny August afternoon with lots of blue sky shining down on the water. Since it was a teacher function, we were all wearing name tags with both our name and our school's name. Being so girly, I hate it when nametags cover my cute sundresses and amazing jewelry.

We all began to group by schools and start our own introductions. This was basically the first meeting of the Victory Street Irregulars. They became my best friends. These memoirs are about our time together as we got to know one another and our assorted adventures in Savannah. It is true that everyone has a story, and having introduced ourselves, it was nice to just go ahead and spill our guts to one another.

Doris came here from Minnesota. She dragged her husband Cane here because he had managed to get himself into a little trouble, and while in court, the Judge gently suggested that he might want to relocate and possibly get married to avoid future jail time. He was a cabinet builder, so Savannah looked like a good place for him to start over. The interesting thing was that he actually went to work for Gulfstream making airplanes. This was something he knew nothing about, so he falsified his resume and told his references what they should say when called. I am standing there in the sunshine thinking, "You have got to be kidding me; seriously?" But he was so smart that on the job he could replicate what he saw others doing. I am thinking, I really can't wait to meet this Cane guy. Doris was so ding dang cute that he must be a hunk to boot.

Eva was a beauty queen from Mississippi (no lie, she was Miss Congeniality in the Miss Mississippi pageant) who also followed her beau, Cary. Both had graduated recently from college and he had a job offer at the Sheraton Hotel, Hilton Head. They were engaged to be married back home that summer, so lunches were optional in order to fit into that special wedding gown. Eva was hired at the last possible moment and had to learn all about fifth-grade curriculum and everything else at the last minute, with no chance to set up her classroom. Thank goodness she is loaded with savvy smarts and determination so that these obstacles were overcome, and the students loved her!

Emma came to us from Augusta, Georgia. An experienced teacher of young students with disabilities, she was hired to teach kindergarten. She followed a fellow as well. 'The Colonel' was a studly West Point graduate and had been hotly pursuing the lovely Emma the year before while he was stationed in Augusta. This pursuit continued when he was transferred to teach ROTC classes at Savannah State University, even though Emma had caught him with another lady. After an avalanche of apology flowers and poetry arrived at her school office, her faculty had convinced her to give him another chance. Thus, she packed her bags, and the Irregulars volunteered to be on high alert to see if this Ladies Man could keep his zipper up.

Now, Vera was our radical gal from Berkeley. She had been teaching and living in Las Vegas, where, unlike California, there were plenty of teaching jobs. She was taking a break from Sin City and her husband, Statman, who was a high school math teacher. The trouble with living in Las Vegas and being adept at math is that eventually the high probability of winning at hold 'em poker sings like Odysseus' Sirens. Vera figured that if she was going to be a Poker Widow, she may as well be in an elegant city by a beach. So she moved, and Savannah became Soap Opera City as we waited to find out if their marriage would mend or end!

We did not get to meet our Speech Language Pathologist, Tamara, the Diva, on the Riverboat because she was already working at Victory Street, bless her heart. We found out later that Tamara came to Savannah to get away from the scars of a broken engagement. As a Speech Language Pathologist by day and a nightclub singer by night, Savannah was a land of opportunity for her.

Of course, I was the North Carolina chick. My story, you already know. I landed in Savannah with my husband so he could work for a law firm. What you don't know is I got my job without even an interview! Since I had the right certification, they hired me sight unseen and wisdom unshared to teach students with behavioral disorders. Later, when I got into the special education department, I learned there were *fourteen* other positions available that they failed to mention. I could have taught learning disabled students. They called my students the BD students, as they had diagnosed behavioral disorders. Also, I was the only one of the newly formed Victory Street Irregulars with a child.

As we were telling our stories, it seemed that drinks were in order. I saw that there was a bar set up – yes, a real bar with liquor! I said for us to beware, that it had to be a trick. They are trying to trick us to see if we drank alcohol and then we will be immediately fired. The other Irregulars just howled with laughter at the NC redneck because of course it was ok to drink on the cruise. We began to sip, stroll, and get to know one another. Who knew that this would be the start of great friendships and great adventures?

The next orientation was to get to Victory Street and learn my way around. Did I mention Victory Street School was a big, red-brick, three-story school, with no air? Because Lord, yes, it was 100 degrees that day! And of course, the classroom I taught in was located on the top floor.

I got to meet my teacher's assistant, Odell, a young African-American man who was too cute for words. He turned out to be a great guy to be teamed up with. We were the *Ebony and Ivory Team.* We started planning our strategy for the opening of school. We would start the day with Class Meetings and we would implement a behavior system of points and incentives. The students would also choose a behavior goal to work on and graph their behavior each day. We prepared a letter to go home to the parents explaining our system and expectations.

As this planning was going on, I got a call to the office that I had a phone call. It was my former neighbor Keith from Macon calling to say that he was flying over to take me to lunch. Yes, he said flying. He flew a plane as a hobby. Flying with Keith while I was in Macon was always an interesting event, including the time we were flying with his instructor and were making a landing. The instructor told us to *assume the position*, that we were going down. I do not mean in the sexual way. We were about to crash, but clever Keith was able to make the landing safely.

When Ms. Hall, the Principal, and Mrs. Pierce, the Secretary, heard the conversation about Keith flying over to take me to lunch, they acted like I was either crazy, a liar, or both. Now, Ms. Hall rolled her eyes around in her head in such a way that it made me think of a fish's eye. She gave The Fish Eye big time over my lunch plan. Well, Keith arrived and we had a fine lunch on River Street and then he flew back to Macon and I resumed working on the classroom. It was a fight to the finish to get everything ready. In North Carolina, we had a week to train and get ready for school opening, but in Savannah, we had one day!

Vera was working madly on her classroom which was also upstairs on the third floor. Her classroom had not been touched all summer, not even swept, and when Ms. Hall asked her how her day was going, she said, "Everything is great *(That part was a lie),* except that my room was a little funky," which I thought was pretty good phrasing given her efforts of cleaning in that heat, instead of prepping for her students who were coming *the next day.* But Vera got The Fish Eye. Ms. Hall objected to the term *funky.* Vera was amazed. What was she talking about? Ms. Hall explained that it meant *bad sex smell.* Vera's immediate reaction was to wonder what Prince would think of that definition, but out loud she only offered an apology about not knowing East Coast dialect variations.

Early on, we got to have our first Parent Teacher Organization meeting. I was so shocked when a parent actually came to the front door of Victory Street School with a beer in his hand. Open containers were not prohibited, even in schools. That was new for this NC redneck too.

Ms. Hall introduced the whole staff to the parents. She called each of us by name and had us stand up. She told the parents what we would be teaching. She introduced me as the BD teacher. After the meeting, one of the parents stopped me and thought I was the VD teacher, you know, like venereal disease, and said, "How do you teach that?" What an introduction to the Victory Street parents!

We all went to our respective classrooms to greet the parents. As you can imagine, they were not beating down the doors to be there. There were very few parents in total, and even less for the BD class, but we did have Adrian's mom. Ms. Hall introduced us to Adrian, a handsome white boy who would also be in Eva's class. His mom was a pharmacist and explained that Adrian had some issues because he had Tourette's syndrome. We also talked about the unique makeup of Victory Street School since it only had fifth and sixth graders who were bused from all over town and kindergarten children from the neighborhood. Adrian had tried *white flight* in a private school, but his *charming* behavior (due to an obvious disability!) quickly got him kicked out. He would be one of the minority white students at Victory Street School. Odell and I assured his mom that we would take good care of Adrian.

Then in came Adam and his mom. He was a great-looking African-American boy who also had not done well in his neighborhood school. His mom warned us that his behavior was very aggressive and at times a problem for her also. Again, we assured her that we would do our best to take care of him.

It was time for us to leave for the evening and get ready to embrace the first day.

Well, of course Fish Eye Ms. Hall gave me yard duty the first day. Talk about anxiety. Our school was in a very rough part of town, and after the buses arrived, we were in lock-down daily. We were surprised Ms. Hall felt safe parking her Mercedes in the school lot, what with all the used needles and condoms. Vera made the mistake of walking her students across the street to take pictures of the school for their pen pals in another city. Ms. Hall literally came running after them, shouting, "You cannot leave the building!" Her Fish Eyes about popped out. There also was no staying late to get ready for the next day. We all left together in the afternoons because the school was locked tight at 4:00 pm.

As I was watching the students get off the buses and keeping an eye on the playground, I saw a woman from the 'hood come up to the school fence and start running a butcher knife up and down the chain-link fence. The sound of metal clanging against metal resonated over the playground. I ran to the office to get them to call 911 and Ms. Hall said, "Oh, that's just Mrs. Booker from across the street sharpening her knives!"

I knew then and there that it was going to be a LONG year.

Did Will Have a Big Nose?

———— ◆ ————

It was time for a big old Friday outing on River Street. The Victory Street Irregulars liked to meet on Friday after school at Spanky's bar. We had to celebrate another week of survival in The Fish Eye workplace. A week's survival really put us in a mood to drink.

We made quite a production, as usual, moving our chairs around. We were trying to choose who should sit where, but had no trouble taking the time to move in a chair for a good-looking man named Will. He had given Tina Dawn, my daughter, swim lessons at the Y in Macon. He also attended Mercer Law School with Paul. He saw me and I just naturally invited him to join us. It was a good thing that even though we were broke in Macon, we were able to pass a few bucks to Will for those swim lessons.

The Y in Macon was really cool. It had a walking track that was above the pool and gym. I could exercise and then walk the track looking at all the good-looking hunks below. There definitely were some hunks there. For example, the guy who checked you in was a centerfold in Playgirl Magazine, for real. He had yellow tiger eyes in addition to a body made for sin. His wife was a second-grade teacher and his actual profession was as a plumber. Can you imagine that plumber coming to your house? He could plumb my pipes any day! Well, his wife is the one who submitted his pictures to Playgirl. Oh well, I digress, as usual.

The usual Irregulars were present, and we were gabbing about our week. Doris leaned over and asked who Will was. I told her how I knew him and about the swim lessons. Now, I already had evidence that Doris had a bit of a wild streak. She had even said that, despite her husband Cane, she would take anybody available and would not hesitate to be with Paul, even though we had become great friends. I knew I was in trouble when Doris said that she would teach Paul piano lessons, and I knew she did not have a piano!

She asked me to introduce her to Will and say that she was into water sports. I introduced Doris as a *lover of water sports.* Then I introduced him to our Diva Tamara, our beauty queen Eva, our Berkeley Vera, and our lovely Emma. We told him a little about Victory Street and I caught him up on Paul and his position with the firm. I am not sure that he heard any of that since he picked up on the *water sports* cue. He left with Doris before the next round of drinks. I later found out that they went to Doris's house and Cane just happened to come home and see them *in flagrante delicto.* Well, that Cane had some cool. He just enjoyed watching, according to Doris. When I told Paul, he was a bit enraged. "How could you do that to Will?" I couldn't help it. I just forgot about Cane!

The next Friday, at our Spanky's drinking adventure, I had Doris reminisce about her time with Will. Tamara interrupted her story to say that Will had a big nose. Doris said, "Well he had a big dick, too" and we all just hooted.

Do Hurricanes Ever Hit Savannah?

———◆———

Another typical Friday afternoon often involved Odell, my teaching assistant, coming home with me after school. Tina Dawn would get home first. She was used to being a 'latchkey kid' from her days in Macon when she was younger.

Getting home first was not a problem for her at all. We had the McHenrys who lived next door; next door as in the other half of our duplex. Well let me tell you that Barbara was the lady of the house and was all about her Pekinese dog. She loved him to pieces. I did not know it then, but I know it now! When she died, we all went to her graveside service – including the dog!!!! To understand more of the neighborly dynamics, let me tell you about her husband, Mr. McHenry. He had Alzheimer's and could not remember shit, seriously. He would go to the grocery store and forget why he was there. The worst of it all was that he and Barbara were raising their granddaughter, Jenny, who was a little younger than Tina Dawn. Get this, Mr. McHenry drove the carpool. Yes, he would forget to take them, forget to pick them up, or pick them up and forget how to get home. It was always a hoot; the girls would mess with him and take his cigarettes and money.

So, back to when we came home (fingers crossed that Tina Dawn would make it there!). Odell would sit down in the living room with Tina Dawn while I got us both a beer. Odell and I would drink our beer while Tina Dawn and I chatted about our day (the good, the bad, the funny, and sometimes the ugly!). Then Odell would finish his beer and leave. Did you notice that he did not talk? He never did. It would amaze Tina Dawn and me both that he would hang, but never speak! I am sure he was enamored with our "girly" conversations! He was cute as a button and we loved him dearly.

This particular Friday, the buzz was all about the hurricane that was coming. Hurricane Bob (yes that was its name!!) was supposed to be a doozy, with 75 mile-an-hour winds and a storm surge. Paul had already talked about all the preparations he would make: filling the washing machine with water, putting boards over the windows, having candles ready and a weather radio nearby. (Notice that Paul wasn't home yet!) Tina Dawn and I decided that we would go to Tybee Island because we had heard there would be hurricane parties. That's right – hurricane parties. Hey, any excuse for a party at the beach was fine by us.

We drove out to the beach and parked there with Bo, the local parking lot attendant. He said that we were a little late but that people were still partying. Sure enough, people were on the beach. The wind and sand were both blowing. How cool was this? Not living at the beach before, Tina Dawn and I had not experienced this. There were people surfing and loving those big waves, riding them all the way in. People were drinking Can Shake/Purple Jesus/Joy Juice, whatever you want to call it. Of course, Tina Dawn just had Sun Drop.

As the evening progressed, the wind picked up something fierce and the sand was whipping around. The sand was blowing into our drinks and that is a no-no. Tina Dawn said, "Mom, what is Paul going to say when he finds out we are not home and a hurricane is coming?" (Paul is Tina Dawn's stepdad.) Yes, it is the seventh-grader telling the mom to have some sense.

We proceed to walk back towards the car. Mind you that we are one of the few remaining! (Hell, even Bo was packed up and gone!!!) The waves were rising higher and higher. Now, to get to where we parked we could walk up on a ledge, and that seemed as good a time as any to watch the waves come in...

When the waves started coming over the ledge, eye-to-eye, Tina Dawn said, "Mom, what is wrong with this picture?" We were lucky to get to the car. I guess that is what they meant by "storm surge." We braved the way home and battened down the hatches for old Hurricane Bob. Fortunately, Bob was not a direct hit on Savannah. We certainly enjoyed all the excitement, but that is enough hurricane for me.

The Goldbergs' Visit

O ur best friends from home in Cherryville are the Goldbergs: Mary, Leonard, Margaret, Alise, and Neal. Paul met Leonard before we were married. Paul went to try out for the lead role in the Cherryville Little Theatre production of *All American*. My dad, the Judge, said that Paul should not try out because he might get the part. Of course, fool that I am, I thought that was the purpose of trying out for a play. Well he tried out and sang *Memory* for his audition and got the part. That day, Leonard, who was directing the play, went home and told Mary that they were going to meet new best friends. We began a great relationship and would get together at Leonard and Mary's every Friday night with Adele and Mason and Louise and other assorted friends. We would drink, laugh, and stay up until I was asleep on the sofa. I just could never do late nights.

Well anyway, Paul and I did obviously get married and did numerous theatre productions with the Goldbergs over the next five years. They even helped us move to Macon, GA. I cried all the way there because I could not imagine being without them. They visited us in Macon several times, so it was a natural progression that they would come to visit us in Savannah.

We decided that we should go on an excursion to Tybee Island so they could have the beach experience with us. Paul made his famous Scurvy Medicine (gin, tonic, and limes – necessary to keep Scurvy and Malaria away) and filled a cooler with beer and a bag with snacks and other beach stuff (especially a vat of sunscreen since all the Goldbergs are pasty white) and we all took off.

Tina Dawn and I, call it fashion weird or what, thought it was a little crazy (or too much Scurvy Medicine) that Mary went swimming in the ocean in her clothes. Us adults embraced the moment and the Scurvy Medicine and proceeded to have a grand old time on the beach. Eventually, the beautiful day was coming to a close and we decided to meander back home. We all packed up our assorted, plentiful beach items and walked toward Bo and the parking lot to get into the Goldbergs' van.

Paul, for some reason, was the driver of the Goldbergs' van. I guess he was the most sober at the time and no one lets 'Yours Truly' Annie drive. (I am the worst driver, drunk or sober makes no difference, and my list of wrecks, tickets, and car mishaps is quite extensive.) We were loaded up, kids toward the back, and Paul began the drive back. An argument ensued between Paul and Mary about either religion, social work (they had both been social workers and Mary was still a social worker at the time) or politics and the more they argued, the madder Mary got. For some reason, unbeknownst to us, Mary took a full beer out of the cooler and propelled it to hit Paul squarely in the head. Yes, he was the driver and promptly ran the van off the road, cursing and in pain. He had to have a moment to recover and Mary took that as her opportunity to escape from the van and wander drunkenly into the marsh.

Of course, Leonard got out and dragged her drunk, wet ass back into the van. We made it home. We all climbed out of the van and went into the house for a cold brew. Paul proceeded to make our favorite company dish: Geechi Stew, or some call it Low Country Boil.

You start with a giant pot of boiling water, add smoked Andouille sausage and let it boil for ten minutes, add Old Bay Seasoning and small red potatoes and the mixture boils for ten minutes. Then add small ears of corn and boil for ten minutes, and finally shrimp. Continue cooking until shrimp turn pink. Paul makes a cocktail sauce that is literally to die for, with lots of horseradish and a little catchup. When the shrimp turn pink, you pour it all out on newspaper on the picnic table with lots of butter and paper towels and begin your company feast.

Well, we *thought* we were beginning our company feast, only to find out that drunk, wet Mary ran off into the neighborhood wearing a t-shirt and white granny panties (she was now angry with Leonard) and of course, she does not live here and does not know the neighborhood and neither does Leonard who is running after her. We had to go after her too and drag her drunk, wet ass back into the house. Yes, a lot of fun was had by all!!!

To culminate this adventure with our wayward friends, Leonard heard a knock at the front door (no it was not his house but he answered the door anyway). He is Jewish and was aghast when the Jehovah's Witness group entered our house to pray over the group. Lord knows we needed it!!!! They were not mystically aware of our sinful day but came back to our house to pray for us because I had made a contribution to them earlier in the week. I thought they were so cute. I had never seen a Jehovah's Witness Group before. Leonard was like – Annie really???

Dungeons and Dragons

———◆———

Since September was ebbing, Odell and I were making plans with the class for what goals and incentives we would set for October. Ms. Hall put a notice in our boxes about the Georgia Arts Festival and how classes and schools could submit potential projects for grants. I am amazed that Fish Eye actually gave information to us!!!! That was a surprise.

Our class decided that they would like to try a grant to earn some bonus bucks for our class incentives. At our class meeting, we discussed things that we were planning and voted on what might make an interesting project to promote. One of the new things we were doing in our Class Meetings was to play an adventure game. In the '70s and '80s, there was a popular adventure game played by young and old alike called Dungeons and Dragons. In this game, there is a Dungeon Master who plans out the dungeon, hence the game. There is no game board and no game pieces. The game actually happens in your mind. You roll the dice to determine the type of character you will be in the dungeon. Will you be a wizard, warrior, dwarf, etc.?

At the Goldbergs', Paul was the Dungeon Master. We still have the master plan and Mary is still 'dead' in a corner. I died several times myself. This was originally a Paul idea that I should introduce my students to the game. He is a great idea man; one of the reasons I keep him.

We bought some dungeon adventure books that were written on a student level. He said it might be interesting that instead of each student gathering experience and treasure for themselves as they navigate the dungeon, they could play as a group. This would build group dynamics and improve their problem-solving abilities. I went with the idea and the students were just beginning to play. We did this at the end of Class Meetings for about 10 to 15 minutes, Monday through Thursday.

The students were excited and thought that this sounded like an award-winning project. I wrote the grant application after school hours, and each time I did a section, I asked for the students' input at the next Class Meeting. The students were delighted when I told them the grant application, Adventure Games: A Way to Improve Group Dynamics, was complete and submitted.

Odell was such a great assistant. He provided encouragement and input. We both kept a record of dungeon activities and how the teams worked together as part of our opening activities. After the journal, the quote for the week, and looking at their behavior graphs, we would discuss ways to cooperate and work as a team to promote group dynamics and skills such as listening, appropriate discussion, and ways to reach consensus. Saying "we are doing this my way, dumbass" was *not* an appropriate way to reach consensus.

Ms. Hall was notified by the Georgia Arts Council that our class won the grant!!!! To receive our coveted award, we had to attend a Principal's Meeting and demonstrate our project: Adventure Games: A Way to Improve Group Dynamics. Our class could not believe this. We were so excited. This would be our first field trip. We prepared our script with everyone having input. Valerie, Shanika, Adrian, and Kendrick were selected to attend. They had all worked really hard on the project and the script for the presentation.

We had to take our script, dice, and the selected adventure book. We also took other adventure books as examples the principals could see. The idea was that they might take this activity back to their schools to try in their classes for students with behavioral disorders. This grant and exhibition was big news at our Department for Exceptional Children, since this type of acclaim was rarely given to our classes. The Department for Exceptional Children was the administrative offices that provided the curriculum and guidance to the teachers of students with disabilities. We lovingly referred to them as *"The Dark Side."* Our Consultant from the Chatham County Department for Exceptional Children planned to attend the Principal's Meeting as well.

To prepare for the Principal's Meeting, during Class Meeting each day, their little group practiced playing the game and using our script. Adrian, who was in Eva's class, worked with her on his part of the script. We knew his mom would have him well dressed and ready for that day. He would be the white student amidst the three black students. He was the brain of the group, but there WAS an issue. Sometimes his Tourette's got the best of him and the cursing would commence. Eva said that he would perform like a champion. She always had Adrian's back!

The big day came. Odell was driving and the fab four were in back. We were rolling along toward the Principal's Meeting. We started to cross the old Talmadge Memorial Bridge. A new bridge was erected in its place in 1990 (Talmadge Bridge website). Kendrick began to kick, scream, and generally go cray cray. Bless Pat, that boy had never been across the bridge. Shanika put the window down thinking air would be good for him. The script blew out the window. Holy Hell ensued.

Odell stopped the car, but we could not retrieve the script. Kendrick tried to bolt out of the car and Odell and I had to restrain him, oh yes, right there on the highway, on a *bridge*. He was fighting us like an octopus. Finally, we got him calm enough to stuff him back in the car. Valerie was giving Adrian the business about how he better not go all Tourette's on the principals since the script went out the window. Well, I didn't know whether to cry, puke, faint or do all three.

We made it to the Principal's Meeting and they had a place for us to wait to be called. Fortunately for us, we did not have to wait long. They ushered us into a great introduction. They had a table set up for us to play. The kids knew the script by heart and we had a lovely time. Fish Eye was beaming out in the audience. We returned as heroes for a day or two at Victory Street School. Eva greeted Adrian with a big hug and her class clapped for him. Kendrick was looking a little embarrassed, but none of the kids ratted him out. It was one of our best field trips ever and the students loved our grant certificate and check to spend on our class.

I submitted a proposal to the Council for Exceptional Children's national conference in New Orleans about our Adventure Games. It was accepted and the Department for Exceptional Children, or Central Office, (or the Dark Side, as we formally call it) made sure that I could attend, expenses paid. This was in spring.

Our friend Louise called and said that she was flying from Cherryville (via Charlotte Douglas International Airport, something we do not have in Cherryville) to Savannah to visit since this was spring break. No problem. She could accompany me to New Orleans and share my room. She only had to get herself a flight to New Orleans and back. Louise flew in to Savannah and Paul and I picked her up at the Savannah airport. We all got in the car to ride to the house and Louise was all nervous from her flight. She lit a cigarette and somehow caught her hair on fire. Paul pulled over. (Seems there is a lot of pulling vehicles over in this memoir.) He put her hair out and we went on to the house with the smell of burned hair lingering. We had a great couple of days there showing Louise Savannah and enjoying a sunny but chilly Easter.

We took Louise out to a bar. Louise and I had a couple of beers and played "Magic Carpet Ride" about 17 times on the jukebox until Paul said it was time to take us away from River Street. Louise asked if she would have to fly over water to get to New Orleans and I said no. What harm is a little white lie to get my Louise to New Orleans with me? I flew out and got to New Orleans first. When Louise arrived, she looked like she had been pulled through a knothole sideways. She had carried on something else on that flight and consumed a lot of liquor when she realized she was flying over water.

Louise and I were staying in the Hilton near the Superdome. That was the convention hotel. Louise was thrilled because she is a sports enthusiast and the idea of the Superdome was awesome to her. The hotel had two towers and we spent a lot of the week lost in the hotel. We could never remember which tower we were in.

I got her into my session at the conference by saying that she was a School Psychologist from Charlotte who worked with me on my idea for Adventure Games: A Way to Improve Group Dynamics. Louise was really a businesswoman. I did my presentation and showed a video taken of the students at the Principal's Meeting. The audience was very enthusiastic and, of course, most of the attendees at my session were teachers of behaviorally challenged children. I saved some time at the end for questions. Most of the questions were directed to Louise, the "School Psychologist from Charlotte." Louise was not a School Psychologist, but she bluffed them pretty well. I was significantly impressed and so was the audience.

After our presentation, some attendees invited Louise and me to a party at the hotel. The group of educators throwing the party was called The Division of the Morally Impaired, otherwise known as DMI. (That was so cute because all the divisions in the CEC had to do with the disability they represent. I was a legitimate member of CCBD, the Council for Children with Behavioral

Disorders.) Of course, Louise and I decided to attend. Wow!!!! What a crazy crowd. The hotel suite was full to the max and people were dressed in their sexiest duds. It turns out that the sexiest ones were awarded a t-shirt with an immoral slogan. Louise and I were told that champagne was in the bathtub. Of course we went into the bathroom, and sure enough the tub was full of ice and bottles of champagne. The problem was that to get to the tub we had to pass several gentlemen, so to speak, with their penises out. That was more of an adventure than taking the fab four to the Principal's Meeting! Well, we did get our bottle of champagne and, of course, I immediately joined DMI and could not wait for the next national convention.

The Corner

———◆———

In Macon, Tina Dawn was a minority and was picked on daily. This was hard for a child who was only eight years old. If she wore a necklace, they would pull it off her neck. Some of the kids would even chase her down the street as she was going home. It was hard on a little kid.

Paul was in law school at Mercer and I was working, so she was a 'latchkey kid.' She wore her house key around her neck and let herself in each day as she came home from school. So when we moved to Savannah, Paul and I agreed that Tina Dawn should get to attend parochial school at St. Paul's Lutheran, which was also the church we attended. Tina Dawn's class only had six students. They looked alike, dressed alike, and were from 'like families.' This specialized situation seemed good for her, and us.

She had a teacher who to this day is her favorite teacher, Mr. Francis. He did the music program and the math program. Now Mr. Francis had this idea that math is exact, you either got a 100 or a 0. I had a big old screaming fit, and Paul too, when she brought those zeros home. Tina Dawn said, "Either you had them all correct and made 100 or if you missed any, you made a zero." So I called the parents to find out and Sally's, Susan's, and Candy's moms all said that is what their children told them. We parents descended on the school in a parental whirlwind of fury, like ugly on an ape, but Mr. Francis would not budge. The kids became good math students, which has certainly served Tina Dawn well in her educational career and work life later on. In Mr. Francis's music program, he believed everyone can be taught to sing and must sing a solo in the chapel. To me, this was more startling than the math grades since neither Tina Dawn nor I can sing. He said everyone can be taught, and Tina Dawn had to sing a solo. She did. That was a big day for us. I asked for a little time off from work to go hear that production.

The church had these great Wednesday night events with classes for adults and children. The big draw was the supper every Wednesday night. You just put a donation in the basket to pay whatever you could, and the food was always good. Everyone in the inner-city neighborhood around St. Paul's Lutheran was welcome. All could come and eat and participate in the activities each week. Their outreach program was noted in The Lutheran magazine.

One of my favorite church activities was co-ed softball. I have always enjoyed sports (I majored in PE in college before switching gears to special education), so I signed up. The first night, I told Paul that I was going to play softball and that after the game we were all supposed to go out to this bar called The Corner. We played a great game. I could hit and run to first base, so I got to be the lead-off batter. We had such a great time. I had never played on a co-ed team before. That added an extra element of excitement.

After the game, I followed some of the players to The Corner. I was shocked. The Corner was a curb outside a convenience store. Yes, literally a curb. We went in the convenience store in our St. Paul's Lutheran uniforms, bought beer, and sat outside on the curb and drank it. It was so well known that pizza could be delivered there. One player had his morning paper delivered there. I had to find a payphone to call Paul. I knew he would not believe this shit. This was amazing. We got pretty rowdy, and as we left, we would bump each other's car bumpers as we drove away. I enjoyed many game nights at The Corner.

Tamara and the Barba Negra

———◆———

The Friday crew of the Irregulars got together at Spanky's after work as usual. We were exhausted and looked a little like warmed-over hell. We all had on our t-shirts, skirts, and sandals. The story of the week was about the trouble I got in with Ms. Hall.

Adrian walked into school as I was doing hall duty up near the front office. I was greeting the students as they came in and monitoring the front door entrance for safety. Adrian was all dressed up in his jeans and a red and black leather jacket. Yes, it is Fall in the South and incredibly hot, but my boys had to wear their leather anyway. I said, "Man, Adrian, you sure look funky today." He smiled and walked to class, where Odell greeted the students and got them started on their morning work.

Ms. Hall came over and called me into her office. I sat down as she closed the door, yes, closed the door; the signal that I was in trouble. She sat down and began to look at me with The Fish Eye. "Mrs. Bell, why did you say that Adrian was funky?"

45

"Well, I did not," I said. "He *looked* funky because he has on that great red and black leather jacket."

"Well, Mrs. Bell, to us at Victory Street School that means that he smells bad."

My jaw dropped. I stared at her a minute. "I did not know that and will be sure to apologize to him."

Can you believe that? You cannot make up stuff like that. If she spent more time checking on Secretary Pierce canoodling with Custodian Floyd in the closet, the front office would have better coverage and the school would be much cleaner. Vera also got called out on the use of that word. I am so glad she did not say "sex smell" to me! I would have croaked. Things in The Fish Eye world keep me confused.

I should say keep *us* confused. Because next, Emma regaled us with her Fish Eye kick story. She and Ms. Hall were at a district kindergarten meeting where the district's proposal for full-day kindergarten classes was being discussed. Thinking that her expertise with young children in low-income areas would be valuable, Emma shared how full-day kindergarten classes improved learning in Augusta schools. That's when she felt her shin being kicked under the conference table. Ms. Hall's contribution was that she did *not* support full-day kindergarten. Later, Emma answered a question with positive information about full-day kindergarten classes and, indeed, was kicked again. Emma looked at Ms. Hall, and Ms. Hall glared her best sideways Fish Eye back at her. Emma never said another word.

We Irregulars decided that the best way to cope would be to go hear Tamara sing on Saturday night at the Hyatt on River Street. We planned to meet there at 8, and the first one there was Doris. She snagged us a table up front. We ordered drinks and enjoyed a pleasant evening of listening to our own Diva singing with a jazz group. She was amazing as usual and dressed to the nines. She had on a black cocktail dress and was showing some tail. She was singing her heart out and the crowd loved her sexy beauty and her songs.

One of the waiters took a liking to Doris, and at the end of the evening our bill seemed greatly reduced. As we were leaving, Tamara asked us to wait on her for the walk down River Street. The waiter also seemed ready to join us. He was to catch up with us as we sauntered down the midnight street. The night was beautiful with lots of stars and still enough people out to keep the party atmosphere flowing. We stopped at an old ship called the Barba Negra. It is usually docked there on River Street. It is an old square-rigger that was used in movies like *The Mother Seton*, *His Name was Mud*, and *The Voyage of the Barba Negra*. There is a plaque nearby to remind tourists of its rich history.

At first we stood around and made up stories about ourselves being on the Barba Negra *back in the day*, with Eva as Queen of the Ship. Naturally this led to dancing around pretending she was Cleopatra. Doris elaborated that we would be taken on the ship as sex slaves, and we began to chant and carry on like we were kidnapped and wondering which pirate would save our *booty* and give us part of the bounty.

Then this tall, dark, and gorgeous man walked up the ladder and onto the deck of the ship. He wanted to know what we were doing out there. He could hear us cavorting around when he was down below. He had this amazing German accent and his name was Bernhard. He said that he and his work colleague owned this three-masted barque and that they used to guide people around the ship and tell them about its history. He invited us below and of course, here go the Victory Street Irregulars below deck. We sat down and he shared his wine with us. We talked and matched each other with wild stories until we girls knew it was time to depart.

Bernhard had been pretty friendly with all of us, but as we got up, Tamara stayed cuddled up with Bernhard. She gave us that look that only the Diva Tamara, still in her *show-my-ass black cocktail dress,* can give. It means "Get the hell on out of here and leave me with this gorgeous man with a German accent." As we were climbing up the ladder and saying goodbye, Bernhard followed us out and told us that he would take good care of Tamara. Emma and Eva murmured that they were not quite sure that was right, but Doris, the waiter, and I were like – Oh my God, way to go Tamara!

We went on our way and departed to our separate homes for the evening. Just another Saturday night for the Irregulars with Tamara as the star.

We never heard the details of their little night adventure, but later she said that he was a lot of fun and was not circumcised.

Surprise Party Goes
Way South

———◆———

The beginning of November always holds the promise of celebrating Paul's birthday. Tina Dawn and I had concocted a great plan for his surprise birthday party. We decided to host a Murder Party. Isn't that the perfect theme to host in a murder house? (Just to remind you, in this house someone was REALLY murdered.) Paul and I have been to a couple of murder parties before and we always have a great time.

Tina Dawn and I purchased the murder party kit from the local bookstore. The kit contained a suggested cast of characters and invitations that told them what they should wear to the party to be in theme. It also included the scripts for all the main characters and a suggested menu for the event.

To give you a nitty-gritty on how murder parties work: The idea is that once the guests are all present, it is announced that a murder has been committed and no one can leave. The investigation begins with the cocktail hour. Each of the characters has certain clues in their script that they are expected to reveal during each course of the evening. After cocktails is appetizers, then meal, dessert, coffee, etc. with the mystery being solved at the end of the evening.

Tina Dawn determined the cast of characters and I made sure they were all willing and able. We also invited additional guests who could also try to solve the murder.

Tina Dawn and I planned the menu and, since this was a surprise party for Paul, we began to hide all the party stuff in Tina Dawn's closet. She was just as excited as I was about the party. We'd never tried to plan a surprise party before. We were forging new territory. Tina Dawn kept cautioning me because I have always been notorious for not being able to keep a secret. I had to get a whipping once in my youth for telling my grandmother about the lovely dress my parents had bought her for her upcoming birthday. We knew that on the day of the party we would have to have somewhere for Paul to go so that we could decorate and do meal preparations. We enlisted the assistance of Barry, one of the lawyers in the firm where Paul worked.

The idea was that Barry would ask Paul to go have a drink after work. They always had to work on Saturdays. Well, the firm where Paul worked expected him to work 24/7 and he had issues with that – imagine. We both did. I always talk about fun and exciting things that we were doing in Savannah and wonder why Paul is not mentioned much – he was not there, he was at work.

Well, the long-awaited day of the party arrived. I was a wreck. Keeping a secret nearly killed me. Paul got up that morning and made a declaration. He was not going to work on his birthday. I almost had a heart attack.

I tried to coax him saying, "What would the boss and other attorneys think if he was not present???" He did not care. He was NOT going. At the top of the stairs, I burst into tears and screamed, "What are we going to do?" We could not get ready for the surprise party if he was home.

"Surprise party???" Oops.

Tina Dawn began to scream about how her mom ruined the surprise and could never keep a secret. Paul, who was in the middle of all the yelling and screaming, began to see that it would be in his best interest to suck it up and go to work.

After Tina Dawn stopped being angry, we began to work furiously to get the decorations and food ready and to transform our real murder house into a party murder house. All was going well. At the appointed time, the guests began to arrive and, man oh man, they were in character and their costumes were awesome! Doris came in sparkly party attire (of course, you know Doris as one of the Victory Street Irregulars).

Vergie came dressed as a slut, her character in the script but not at all in real life. Vergie and Tim were friends of ours from Macon. Paul and Tim went to Mercer Law School together and were now both attorneys in Savannah. Vergie and Tim were the ones who suggested that we rent a duplex in their neighborhood. They neglected to mention that a murder had occurred there. Julie arrived in a lovely cocktail dress with pearls. Barry was not with her. He was working with Paul at the firm. They often had a drink after work. Barry knew he was supposed to keep Paul busy so that we could get the guests in place for the surprise. Julie was in a lively mood and eager to help Tina Dawn and I entertain the other guests. Ron was dressed in lederhosen, which was perfect since his character was a hiker. His wife Rise was also present. We met Ron and Rise when we bought our beagle, Opie Sugarlips. I knew Rise as a science teacher in Chatham County Schools. We also joined the same gym. When we went to buy our beagle, he ran up to me, cocked his leg, and peed right on me. Rise was screaming and trying to intervene. I had on a red and white polka dot dress and white lacy socks. I guess he could not resist someone who looked like a fire hydrant!

Buck's character was a plantation owner, which was perfect since I called him "Big Daddy." You have already heard a tale or two about Buck and Lois.

We had a varied assortment of people and script characters having a drink and waiting for "surprise time." It got later and later and no Paul. Except for Tina Dawn, we were all going to be drunk before Surprise Boy got there! Tina Dawn was about to have a cow. Julie called Barry and the boys were having so much fun at the bar after work that Barry forgot the time. Later Paul told us that he kept dropping hints like, "don't we need to be somewhere?" They finally got to the house two hours later!

Barry came dressed as a surgeon for his character in the script. The party commenced and at each juncture, clues were revealed. Tina Dawn and I were in the kitchen finalizing the dinner course when Barry, the Surgeon, came rushing into the kitchen. "Annie, where did you find these people? Are they actors?"

"Barry, what in the hell are you talking about?"

Barry said, "How do they know what to say to give clues? Where do they come up with this shit?" It turned out his script was blank. (There again, who can make this shit up, and what about the funniest person to have a blank script!) He was drunk and making shit up to go along with everyone else!

The night went on and Vergie, the Slut, began to get loud and obnoxious. She did not want to be the killer. As the party progressed, all the characters shared clues and tried to solve the murder. The truth is that I was whipped into a frenzy by the madness of the party. Paul arriving late, trying to feed the guests and keep them on track with the murder, and Barry, the Surgeon, not even having a script. I was drunk and, to this day, cannot even remember who the murderer was. Fortunately, Vergie was not the killer and neither was Barry. The night was a huge success, thank God. Murder party kits are awesome!

Thanksgiving with Mom and Dad

———◆———

November meant that it was the end of the grading period and time for report cards to go out. In Chatham County, teachers were required to use a certain formula for report card grades. One-third was the daily grade, one-third was test grades, and one-third was a score that came from the county test. Incredibly tedious to calculate. It was 1984, so it's not like technology could even be of help. Lotus 1-2-3 was the killer spreadsheet app, and only Vera had a computer, which was a Tandy TRS-80 with a cassette tape recorder for memory! Pass the calculators, please. While supporting each other at Emma's house with libations and indulgent refreshments made the scoring more palatable, we were disgusted to eventually discover that the District policy was a charade. Nobody actually verified teachers' grading processes, so most teachers calculated their students' grades just using combined test scores. Silly us, buying into that ridiculous scheme.

We were further aggravated by the science program's well-coordinated design system – NOT! Items for science experiments came in whether or not you were ready for them. The district had invested in a hands-on science program that automatically mailed the materials needed for experiments to the school so that teachers did not have to go out and purchase the products themselves. HOWEVER, Ms. Hall did not assign a science coordinator to ensure that teachers were following the timeline and reading the preparation materials. The Irregulars did not know a Science Teacher's Manual even existed until the second quarter. That meant that the crickets, frogs, seeds, soil packets, etc. arrived whether or not teachers had the lab equipment or anything else ready to use. The live items died, and the other items got stacked up randomly in a supply room. When the district test day came, students had to take the test whether or not those objectives had been taught. Vera, Doris, and Eva were especially thankful to find the Teacher's Manuals so that the live plants and animals could thrive and help make their large classrooms exciting places of learning.

Speaking of thankfulness, my parents decided to come partake in Thanksgiving with us. They flew into the small Savannah airport. They looked a little worse for the wear coming in from Cherryville by way of Charlotte. We decided Maw Maw and Paw Paw needed drinks from the bar. We sat down and Paul got a scotch, I got my gin martini, Tina Dawn got her Shirley Temple, and Mom and Dad got their white wine. Things were going well, until Dad started to tell a tale about me from my college days.

I had had quite the attractive boyfriend, Ted. Now he was prone to do some drugs and loved to shoplift.

(I know you are thinking he was a thug, but he grew up to be a fine, upstanding man.) We were out with another couple, smoking joints and drinking beer. There was a big hardware store in Cherryville on Highway 150 that had a sign that said "Dixie Lumber – Merry Christmas." It was after midnight and we all four hid behind trees on Highway 150 like the stoned, drunken fools that we were. When the coast was clear and no cars were coming, we dashed out, took the letters off the sign, and hid again. Then we dashed back out and put letters back on the sign, resulting in, "Dixie Lumber Say Shit." We were so proud of ourselves.

The next morning, I got up and went to the table in our bright sunny kitchen all decorated for Christmas and sat down with Mom and Dad. My dad looked up and said that he heard that Dixie Lumber had a *new sign*. I 'bout fell out. I just sat there waiting for the ax to fall, imagining a ton of punishment in my Christmas future. Nothing else was said. Dad went on with his usual Christmas discussion about Joseph and how he believed that Mary was not a virgin. Really??? Now my dad was one of the county district judges, and this discussion always seemed funny to me but I did not even snicker this time.

As my dad retold the story of Dixie Lumber's *new sign* in the Savannah Airport bar for the first time in twelve years, he added some pertinent information. Ted's grandma, who owned Dixie Lumber, had called him at the crack of dawn that morning. She was, as they said, a formidable woman (that means she was mean as hell) and she was screeching about her precious sign and the disgrace that it was to the community with everyone seeing it out on Highway 150 and right at Christmas too. She admonished him that it had my name and Ted's all over it. My dad just listened and said that he did not know a thing about it. Ted promptly fixed her sign and put chicken wire over it so that an awesome misdeed such as this could not be replicated. Yes, it was the best stunt of my life to this day. We all sat in that small airport bar and laughed our asses off. Mom was aghast, saying her favorite thing, "How unfortunate!" while the rest of us continued to laugh. I was a little worried about Tina Dawn hearing about this prank, but what the hell.

Christmas Wishes

———◆———

The beautiful live oaks in Savannah give the feel of the hardwood trees that surround my home in Cherryville. People also begin to decorate for Christmas right after Thanksgiving, just like they do at home. We were so excited to purchase a live wreath for our front door. It made the outside of the house look festive. We did not decorate a lot inside since we knew that we would travel to North Carolina the week of Christmas to spend time with our families. Even Paul was going to get a few days off for Christmas.

It is difficult to remain focused on school during the holidays. We teachers and students are mostly in survival mode anticipating the holidays. Now, Ms. Hall was prone to have these exhausting staff meetings. Our beloved "Fish Eye" had one of her incredibly rambling, unorganized faculty meetings one afternoon in the middle of December. We were all squirming in our seats because she literally held us captive, as a power trip. It was not like we were making a ton of money teaching there. Teachers had second jobs and children in daycare where they had to pay $10 for every 10 minutes past pickup time. It was disrespectful, especially during the month of December when we all had so much to do to be ready for the onslaught of Christmas.

Finally, as she was ending the meeting, she casually mentioned that there would be a Christmas door decorating contest. There would be judges coming around to determine the winners, and it would occur at the end of the next week, right at dismissal time prior to vacation. Wow, Fish Eye came up with a winning idea for Christmas right when we least expected it, but had so little time to carry it out.

All the classes were excited. Of course, Emma, our Irregular teaching kindergarten, was quite enthusiastic. Little people love to do art. Emma had the most unique kindergarten situation that I had ever seen. Victory Street only had neighborhood kindergarten, with bused fifth and sixth grade. I have to keep mentioning that because I just could not accept it. Emma came into her classroom one day and found hypodermic needles in one of the desks. No, she did not have a diabetic student. That had to have been some of the older students stashing them there. We never really knew. She just called Custodian Floyd, spiriting him away from Secretary Pierce, to come and get them and clean the desk. While he was at it, it would have been nice if he could have found a way to get the black mold off the ceiling. Even with those distractions, the little people sallied forth with their learning and made decorations for Emma's door.

I went home in a fit of fury as usual after one of Fish Eye Brown's endless staff meetings. I told Paul and Tina

Dawn about the Christmas door contest. They wanted to wander around the mall a little and grab a sandwich for dinner so off we went.

The mall was abuzz with the holiday shoppers. Tina Dawn had lots of things she wanted to look at and dream about for Christmas. Paul kept telling her she better be good and make good grades or her only Christmas visit would be from the Christmas Toad. That was a white plastic toad that often found its way into the car to Cherryville to be put in her stocking. (It appeared many times over the years. Hell, Tina Dawn is now in her forties and that toad still comes!)

While looking from store to store, Paul noticed at Hallmark that you could get a door cover that looked decorated for Christmas. It happened to be on sale, so we purchased it. Voila!!! I was pleased and could now enjoy my weekend without worrying about what Odell, the kids, and I would do to decorate the door right here at the end of December for Fish Eye's all-of-a-sudden Christmas damn door decorating contest!

Odell and I told the kids during our Class Meeting that we needed to decorate our door for a big Christmas Door Contest. Now what we did was put the Christmas door cover on the door, Odell added some lights, and the kids embellished the Christmas tree on the door cover with paper ornaments. Then we were done and could go outside for a break on the playground. (Did I mention that this was a GENIOUS idea? ☺)!!!

Now, Berkeley Vera had to be her usual radical self, even at Christmas in the DEEP South, and had her students do a Hanukah door. Imagine how that went over. Yeah, like a lead balloon. Of course, she had no fear of Ms. Hall (A.K.A. Fish Eye) bringing her large girth to the third floor.

Eva had her kids busily working on the Christmas door. She told them if they did a quick and decent job on the door that they could all go out to the playground. Adrian told all those chaps to get busy because he wanted to go outside. He already had to do a door for Bell's class. They decorated their door, from scratch of course, and then ran out to the playground.

Adrian was running as fast as he could so that he could join us and ran *slap* into the monkey bars and knocked his fool self out. Adam ran to the office and told Secretary Pierce to call an ambulance. I was running right behind him. The kids were wild, and Eva was too. She had tears and mascara running down her face. (It did piss me off that she was beautiful even with that mess on her face.) Odell was trying to talk to Adrian, but he was out. His mom had been called and was to meet us at the hospital. The ambulance pulling into the playground made quite a spectacle. Odell got in the ambulance with Adrian and off they went to the hospital.

It turned out that Adrian had a mild concussion but would be OK. His mom just needed to keep him home to rest the next day. Boy was he surprised when he returned and saw the big blue ribbon on our door. We won first prize! Yes indeed, with a store-bought door. We were thrilled and Odell and I acted like big shots with our winning class who all got free ice cream! (And even this is funny because who gives an ice cream party in DECEMBER?) Adrian said that the next best news was that Eva's class, his other class, had won second prize and got a red ribbon. He said that he had the prettiest teachers at Victory Street School and that Odell didn't look bad either. It was a good way to close school for Christmas break.

Winter Brings Out the Best in the Irregulars

---◆---

Emma made sure 'The Colonel' was included in the Irregulars' activities when he was not buried in his schoolwork at Savannah State, where he majored in military science.

I don't know whether this only happens in the South, but all manner of critters seem to move inside. I don't just mean two-legged creatures looking for warmth. Emma began to have a rodent problem in her house.

She had The Colonel doing some surveillance for her since she had a stalker ex-boyfriend. With all of The Colonel's raw beefy frame and his military intelligence, he was perfect for scaring off the stalker whenever he came in range of Emma's front porch. Well, of course, since The Colonel was protecting her and all, she did invite him in.

Now, Emma did not want to confront her ex, but she was not at all afraid of the rats. She was trapping them right and left and if one was trapped alive, she just grabbed her gun, took the trap outside, and shot the rat. She was beginning to get quite a collection outside of dead rats.

This particular evening, The Colonel completed his surveillance and was in the kitchen talking to Emma, Doris, and Tamara when a rat ran across the kitchen floor. The Colonel, military science giant, screamed like a woman and jumped up on a kitchen chair while Emma chased the rat outside with a broom. This tickled Tamara and Doris. They could not stop laughing at The Colonel and he began to laugh at himself right from his standing position on the kitchen chair. Emma and The Colonel began to develop a romantic relationship and moved into an apartment together. It was a good thing that they had both become experts in pest control because their new apartment was full of groundhogs. The Colonel and Emma killed all the groundhogs in their apartment and the final total was 31 groundhogs. What does one do with all those dead groundhogs? Doris, our idea woman, said they should just take them to the graveyard. Nobody in there will mind.

At Victory Street, Winter was pretty calm, even with my boys. While I was away at the conference in New Orleans, Odell and the students had captured a huge cockroach. Yes, I said captured. They put him in a cage, labeled with his name "G.R." for German roach of course. I immediately said that G.R. had to be returned to the wild.

About that same time, I noticed that a crystal bear was missing from my desk. Yes, I had committed the cardinal teacher sin, I had a personal item in the classroom. I called an emergency Class Meeting and all the boys and girls went to their desks. I made a speech about how well I thought our class was doing, how our number of office referrals was way down, and that we were becoming a great class, but that now someone from our group had stolen the crystal bear from my desk. At this point, I had a giant lump in my throat and was about to cry. I removed myself from the area and went into time out. I just did not want to ball in front of the class and Odell.

As I was sitting there, I heard one of the boys say, "OK class, empty your pockets. We're buying the teacher a damn bear." It was the most unlikely voice. It was Adam. I could not believe it. I managed to rejoin the group and send the students back to their respective afternoon activities. As it turned out, the crystal bear was recovered. It had been stolen by a student in another class.

50 Shades of Purple

———•———

Odell and I decided to video the kids conducting their Class Meetings. We were planning a Magic Show for the Spring Very Special Arts Festival. The kids were trying to come up with the lineup of tricks to go with *A Day in the Life of a Magic Kid*, being as we considered our accomplishments pretty magical.

We were first going to practice performing for Victory Street classes before our big performance at Forsyth Park. When we performed for the classes, Adrian shot fire out of the magic wand to start the show, and the fireball went right into Olive Oyl's hair!

Olive Oyl was one of the sixth-grade teachers who was very thin and wore her hair pulled straight back into a bun. She looked for the world like Olive Oyl from the old Popeye cartoons. She started out with a really rough class because, like when Eva, our beauty queen, came in at the last minute from Mississippi, the other teachers were supposed to give some of the good kids from their rosters to them, but you know how teachers are. They gave them the roughest students. Leadership and support from Ms. Hall for these new teachers – not!

Anyway, one of my favorite memories of Olive Oyl was when she wanted us all to go out to the playground so her students could show off their science projects. A group of her boys had made a volcano. (Every science fair has to have a volcano, right?) Unbeknownst to Olive Oyl, they had added combustible black powder to their volcano. Man, that thing blew up *good*! It singed Olive Oyl's eyebrows.

I love to reflect back on the Magic Kids. Odell and I were brave taking them to perform in public. It was a beautiful day at Forsyth Park, one of Savannah's beautiful city parks, and Odell and I both had on tuxedos. With the kids dressed in black, we looked sharp. Adam was to perform the Mind Reader, our most difficult trick. Adam was trembling like a leaf in the wind. He said, "Mrs. Bell, you know how people say there are butterflies in their stomach? Well they are really in mine flapping around."

Odell said, "Oh no, I am scared too! Bell, we are not the Magic Kids, we should be called the Magic Chickens!"

Now, back to the video. As we played back the video of our Class Meeting, we noticed that Crazy Kendrick, who was supposed to be working independently, was shooting the bird. That looked *real special* on our video. Adrian started to yell at Kendrick for messing up our video.

Odell tried to calm Adrian down and got his clock cleaned. Oh yes, he hit my Odell right in the eye! I could not believe it. That succeeded in calming the class down. Adrian had scared the shit out of himself because he knew he was in big trouble. Adam said, "Man, we may be crazy kids in here, but we don't hit the teachers."

I sent Odell to the office to report the incident to Ms. Hall. He also went to the cafeteria. Now those cafeteria ladies loved our Odell. He was a Muslim, so they cooked him alternative lunches. No red beans and rice and Savannah sausages for Odell. He had this beautifully baked chicken made just for him. Well, on this particular day, they took out a piece of that frozen chicken and put it right on Odell's black eye to ease that purple swelling and bruising.

When Odell came back to the classroom, he said, "Bell, you will not believe this." I am thinking, *there is more to this day?*

"You know Vera from the top floor (you know her as Berkeley Vera)? She had on this cute short skirt today and Ms. Hall sent her home. Yes, ma'am, sent her ass home to change clothes."

It was not like Vera lived next door to the schoolhouse. Why, she lived on Wilmington Island, thirty minutes round trip. But yes, she went home and took off that cute little skirt, changed clothes, and came back. Vera later noted that the difference between Las Vegas and Savannah teacher dress codes was that apparently in Savannah, it was scandalous to go three inches above the knee, but females could show all the cleavage they wanted in their spaghetti-strap sundresses, which was not OK in Las Vegas, where they wanted to stay far away from the ubiquitous bimbo billboard images.

That afternoon, we were all in the lounge prior to our dismissal. Doris and Vera both had yeast infections. They figured they must have gone to the same gynecologist because they claimed that the medicine turned their private parts purple. I said, "Hold it right there! You did not have to pay all that money for medicine. You could have just hopped up on that counter over there and put your privates right on that ditto machine, turned a couple of go-arounds and voila! Purple privates."

Every teacher knows you were practically purple all over every time you ran copies. Once again, I had doubled over the Irregulars with laughter.

I continued, "Just think, Vera, you tried to show off some purple today with your California mini-skirt, but Fish Eye sent your hips right to the house. Odell even had a purple eye today. I guess purple was the color of the day today at Victory Street School!"

Savannah Is Famous for St. Patrick's Day

---◆---

With the large Irish population in Savannah, St. Patrick's Day was a huge deal, and Paul and I were so excited. Theme is everything and here is a town dedicated to this celebration. We even got the day off! Odell's signature drink of the day was the Fuzzy Navel.

The parade began at 7:30 AM. Paul had a place to park because of the law firm. His sister Dawn (Tina Dawn is named for her) and brother-in-law Jimmy came. Paul always said we sure had a lot of long-lost friends and relatives once we moved to Savannah because everyone came to visit. You could tell it was a great city because everyone wanted to experience it.

The parade route was so crowded that the people moved you. Everything was green. They even dyed the river green. The crowd was loud but fun. As Tamara said, you would buy a beer and drink it standing in the porta-john line. I was so glad that Tina Dawn had friends to hang out with so that we adults could get a little crazy. We actually got into Kevin Berry's Pub, which was surprising with the crowd. The waitress even did her 'Paul usual' which was to say that someone ordered a black and tan they did not want. I acquired a button from someone that said "Fuck Me I'm Irish" but put it in my pocket and only showed it at certain, appropriate times.

Dawn and I were impressed with the fancy porta johns. They had mirrors and sinks. While in the bar, the women took over the men's room. I learned that I had skills I never knew I had. The poor men were left to go in the alley if the porta john lines were too long.

The other Irregulars were hanging out on the river, literally. Eva's husband Cary had a boat and so did Diva Tamara. It was perfect: partying from the water where they could see the crowd without having to be in it. Tamara could not believe that as she watched the parade, a float came by with Bernhard, the *specifically described* hunk from the Barba Negra, laughing, waving to the crowd, and playing the accordion.

Tamara was the master of the boating scene for our group. She had her LeBaron convertible to get the group to the dock at the tiny city of Thunderbolt on the Wilmington River. She looked so damn cute in her convertible. The Thunderbolt marina had a boat we would all laugh at; *The Bofus.* We would say, "It ain't his'n and it ain't mine, it belongs to the bofus."

Tamara had a ploy. She would take her boat out on the water, remove the motor cover, and appear stranded. Sure enough, men would stop to offer assistance to the attractive, stranded lady. They wanted to be her Knight in Shining Armor and she welcomed them with open arms. The boat mysteriously cranked after the man fingered the carburetor a few times. Now, if the man met Tamara's criteria, he was offered a ride in her boat. If he did not, he was on his way in his own boat. Paul, Tina Dawn, and I went on one excursion with Tamara and had a nice picnic on a private island – Dafuskie Island. The island is located between Hilton Head and Savannah. It is the southernmost inhabited sea island in South Carolina. We passed a large boat, and Tamara just happened to have met the owner on a prior adventure. He said that he had purchased the boat at a police auction. His boat had been the communication boat for a drug fleet. He showed us aboard and the large computers were still in there. We were amazed. Tamara was just like a guide along the water, due to her numerous escapades.

Back to St. Patty's Day downtown. Emma and The Colonel had two soldier friends from Fort Gordon who came down for the festivities. They decided to take the bus downtown so no one would have to drive. The guys had their share of green beer during the parade, and when it was over, they all sat on the curb to wait for a bus. Emma was watching the drunk, crazy crowd and not paying attention to the guys. When she realized they were on the wrong side of the street to catch the return bus, she turned around to tell them they needed to cross the street, but all three had laid down on the sidewalk and were passed out with their feet stretching out into the street. It was a task to get them up. She would get two up and one would lay back down. After she managed to get all three up and moving, they were staggering so much that it seemed like an eternity to shovel them onto the bus.

I am not sure to this day how we got my crew home. None of us can remember who was driving. We think maybe it was Paul. We got home and I went upstairs to get ready to go to the big bash our softball team was having. That is the thing – after the parade and all the goings-on downtown and on the river, people were also having private parties. I came downstairs all ready to go and Dawn, Paul, and Jimmy were all passed out in the den. I had to go to the party all by myself.

Of course, Paul had to go to work the next day, even though it was a Saturday. Well, Dawn, Jimmy, and I decided to go back to River Street. We shopped a little and all that shopping made us thirsty. We went into the Long Branch. It was sort of a dive with a lot of men hanging out and drinking. Dawn and I were the only girls. Jimmy was in good company. We got pitchers of Long Island Tea and were having a great time. I began to tell stories. I was telling the story about being in a Washington DC titty bar called the Chesapeake House. The woman dancing was extremely talented. She could make her privates move and she would say, "It's talking to you Baby," as she danced around the men and snapped her *lower lips*. Yes, she had a snapping v-jay-jay. We just called her the *Red Snapper*; it was a seafood house. That was so amazing.

I guess I was a little loud and scary because when we looked up, we were the only ones left in the Long Branch. Again, we are not sure who drove us back to the house for Paul to find us passed out when he came home.

Our Canary Did "Sing Sing"

———◆———

D oris had a great idea. She decided we should do "wig night" at the Sheraton at Hilton Head. We knew that our Diva was singing that night. We all bought cheap wigs and put on our cocktail dresses and headed out. The Sheraton had a popular night club and was crowded that night.

Now Tamara, our tart, looked gorgeous in her black, sparkly cocktail dress. During breaks, Tamara would come over and chat with us. She could not believe the wigs. We thought we looked like rock stars; not so much. We were having our cocktails when I looked up and here came a waitress with a whole tray of B52's. Wonder who that is for? Well, that Doris had ordered them for us. Oh my. *What a night.* Tamara was on the job and could not drink. She was the consummate entertainer. We could not believe that by day she was the speech therapist who helped our students and supported us and by night she shone like a star.

It came time for us to leave. We were so glad that we had The Colonel who was not too drunk to drive us.

He was always such a sport putting up with our shenanigans. Emma was so good to share him with us. Paul was always working and did not get to be part of wig night. Eva's Cary worked for the Sheraton, training in accounting. He did not want to spend his Saturday nights there even on wig night.

Little did we know that after we left, our Diva bellied up to the bar. Immediately a handsome man joined her and began to buy her drinks. She was enjoying his company and did not really want to go home alone. One thing led to another and he got in the car with Tamara. Unfortunately, the cops had set up a sting operation to catch us drunks leaving the Sheraton. The cops pulled Tamara over. She was quite drunk and she did not want the guy to be involved since he was a married man and there was no need for him to be in trouble. She refused to tell them the gentleman's name. They became hostile and said that they would just "throw the book at her." She would not relent and motioned for him to leave. He exited the car.

The cops took our Diva to the jailhouse and towed her car. She was charged with Driving under the Influence and was put into the drunk tank in the Beauford jailhouse with 4 other ladies (and I do use that term loosely). Tamara described them as "seedy." "Seedy girls talking trash." Tamara said they were dirty and smelly. Imagine that. They were out on a Saturday night and were not wearing sparkly cocktail dresses in the jailhouse. Tamara used her one phone call, not to call one of us Irregulars, but to call her boyfriend Moby. Moby was a true-blue good guy. He had to go get Tamara's car because she had another gig on Sunday night at a different venue. He had to bring all her audio equipment and her next lovely outfit. She spoke of that next outfit fondly.

Tamara, who could not drink with us at night, could drink during the day. She loved to have a drink or two at the Sheraton and then saunter across the street to Lady Jane, this fabulous expensive boutique. Now, drunk shopping is way more fun, but not the best idea because one tends to max out their credit card. Well, Tamara bought the great outfit Moby would pick up for her during a drunk shopping excursion, but she also bought a cool-as-shit London Fog trench coat that she has to this day. Well I guess you have probably figured out that the next Friday afternoon, Tamara had the story of the week!

Mirror, Mirror on the Wall, Who is the Fairest of Them All?

———◆———

J ust another morning with the alarm going off. I ran in to sing the Uppy Duppy Song to Tina Dawn. She is NOT a morning person and my singing really sets her off.

I went into the bathroom naked to wash my face, brush my teeth, etc. The sink was a pedestal sink with a mirror over it. As I brushed and rinsed, honestly, for *no* reason, the mirror shattered into a million pieces. I, being so polished and in control, yelled "FUCK." I was covered with glass.

Paul and Tina Dawn came running into the bathroom going, "What the Fuck?" A whole lot of fuck was going on. I was bleeding and Paul was a little concerned. He ordered Tina Dawn to get a broom. The two of them were trying to get the glass off me and sweep it up before any more injuries could occur. Finally, after the fucks settled and the blood was cleaned up, we could see that, believe it or not, I only had one deep cut on the knuckle of my right hand. Amazing, go figure, man was I lucky.

Now, that Paul is a major person to have around during any disaster. He got a whiffle ball and cut it in half. He put it over my knuckle and taped it right good. Paul and Tina Dawn helped me get into some underwear, pants, and a shirt. Tina Dawn got ready for school and took off to the carpool while Paul took me to the Emergency Room. Fortunately we had not been there before, but I knew that there was an Emergency Room employee who would *not* be assisting us.

Just a couple of weeks back, there was a huge party in Savannah's Historic District that Paul the big-shot attorney was invited to and, of course, could bring his very lovely wife. Paul is not the social creature he should be to advance his lawyerly career, and after Julie (the wife of Barry, an attorney in the firm with Paul) and I got into the coat closet at the last party and modeled rich women's furs, he was less than enthusiastic to attend. Well, fine. I had a softball game anyway.

As it turns out, during this party-to-not-be-attended, there was Drinking and Cavorting going on. Two men were having a special session of love-making in one of the bedrooms that involved *muskrat love*. What is that? Well that is when a small rodent, in this case a gerbil, is placed in a tube that is then inserted into one of the gent's most private places. The theory, and believe me I do not know from personal experience, is that the little gerbil will flutter around and provide a satisfying feeling. Now, the problem in this case is that the gerbil would not come out. Thus, those gents had to make a trip to the Emergency Room.

One of the Emergency Room staff was aghast. Remember, these gents were part of the movers and shakers and important people of Savannah. I am not mentioning any names, but she recognized them immediately, and when she saw the nature of the problem, she excused herself and went out to call others to tell this tale. That indiscretion on her part got her fired. So *she* would not be helping me in the Emergency Room.

And, man oh man, was I mad that I was not at that party!!!! And to think, we at Victory Street consider ourselves Irregulars.

Back to my sojourn in the Emergency Room. The doctor was quite impressed with the way that Paul dressed the wound. He sewed up my knuckle and we were good to go. I still look at that scar with memories. Paul and I both had to go to work. When I arrived at Victory Street, it turns out that Pierce told Odell via intercom that I had an accident and would not be there. The boys were trying to guess what might have happened to me. They decided that I was out in the softball outfield saying, "I got it, I got it!" and then I *really* got it.

I thought that all my Irregulars would be there to say, "Poor, poor baby," but it was not to be. Tamara was not there that day. Berkeley Vera did a little bit of, "poor baby," but was more like, "Put on your big girl panties because we need to come up with a quick gift! Didn't you notice both Doris and Emma were absent?" Doris and Emma had planned to be absent for a huge event in the life of the Irregulars. The Colonel had gotten Emma pregnant, and he had begged her to marry him. It did take some begging, let me tell you. She was fine with not being married, but he was not. He kept saying that it just wasn't fair. He said that Emma only had him around to be a sperm donor. She claims that to this day she cannot remember their anniversary.

He finally talked her into it, and this was the big day. Emma had really wanted a baby. She kept saying that at the ripe old age of 34, her biological clock had started BANGING. The timing was not great, but is it ever? The Colonel decided that if Emma was in a *yes* mood, he better get this deed done pronto. They needed a witness, so Emma, The Colonel, and Doris went to the Justice of the Peace for the wedding. It was simple but sweet.

They were standing there together listening to the Judge when the Judge said, "We are gathered here together between God and Doris" and The Colonel started to laugh. Guess the Judge did not realize how funny that sounded. The Judge stopped reading and admonished The Colonel right there in the middle of the ceremony and told him that this was a serious matter. Emma said that the serious matter took all of ten minutes.

Now I ask you, who is the fairest of them all?

Why Was Cane Arrested?

———◆———

Got a call from Doris one night. Cane had been arrested and she had to go to a bondsman to try to get him released. There was an additional problem. The keys to his car were in a leather jacket and being kept by a barmaid at a local bar. Doris was mad! She said that she was coming to pick me up. I am amazed, in retrospect, that Paul agreed to remain at home with a sleeping Tina Dawn on a school night. I am sure that I must have said something simple like "Doris is coming to get me to help her with a school project" or something.

Anyway, the next thing I knew I was in the car with Doris. She was fuming about this barmaid and how we were going to get out the can of butt whip and drag her out of the bar and whip her ass in the parking lot until she gave us the leather jacket and car keys. As we were driving to a bar in a rough part of town, I asked Doris what we were going to do if this was a BIG woman. She may have a large economy can of butt whip. I felt we should have a plan B. Doris was so mad at her husband Cane for being so stupid that she could not see past her can of butt whip.

As we pulled into the parking lot, I began to feel really nervous. Two teachers should not be going into a bar to whip ass on a school night. The thought of being fired did enter my mind. Making the news also entered my mind. Joining Cane in the slammer and needing a bondsman also crossed my mind as we crossed the parking lot and entered this dark, grungy bar.

A girl walked out from behind the bar toward Doris and me. I high fived Doris and said, "Look, she's a little troll. We can do this!" The girl walked up to Doris and handed over the leather jacket with the keys in it without a word being spoken. We were done and all was right with the world.

We took Cane's loot and left immediately without looking back. Doris was putting the jacket in the car when she discovered a vial of white powder in the jacket. Wow, I had never seen cocaine in my life.

Just seeing it was scary to me. There again those thoughts of losing my job and being arrested came back into my head. Doris was just happy that *she* had the vial and vowed that Cane was not getting that back. That would be his punishment for being arrested and for being with the little troll barmaid.

Doris, in her wicked mode, had been waiting for the right time to utilize that prize cocaine she found in Cane's jacket. It just so happened that Paul was going out of town for the weekend for some law adventure. Tina Dawn was going to be staying with friends and Doris was to come pick me up on Saturday morning. When she got to the house, we snorted the coke. Yes, right there at the coffee table in my den. We felt so cool, just like rock stars. I even went upstairs and put on Tina Dawn's pink satin jacket. Doris wanted to go to the mall. We were high as kites, yes we were.

As we were leaving the house, we managed to lock my beagle, Opie Sugarlips, in the car with the keys. One of my favorite visions of that miss-spent day is Doris looking in the window of the car and thinking she could teach Opie Sugarlips to pull the lock up and open the door. That was when I went back into the house and called a locksmith. We were literally dancing in the street when the locksmith arrived and got Opie Sugarlips and the keys out of the car. We put the dog in the house. We would not be deterred from our trip to the mall.

For some reason, Doris just *had* to go into the pet store at the mall. Well that was fine with me. What I did not anticipate was her letting the animals out of their cages. I rescued a couple of goldfish and put them in my pockets as we exited the pet store. I really do not remember much about that day except that both sets of my lips were numb, if you catch my drift. I now know why people get addicted to cocaine!!!!

Tina Dawn was less than pleased when she found dead goldfish in her satin jacket. And when Paul asked about my weekend, I just said it was fine and that I missed him. We still cannot remember, to this day, why Cane was arrested, but Doris said he would have just lied about it anyway.

Beach Tales

———◆———

Tybee Island comes alive in the spring. People seem to just come over the dunes to play whenever it was a bright, sunny day. Doris and I tried to lay out one day during spring break, but it was so cold, we ended up covered in sand and rolled up in our beach towels.

Tybee Island is so close to Savannah, just a quick jaunt down the oak tree- and Spanish moss-lined Victory Drive. Back at home in North Carolina, going to the beach was a rare vacation and a considerable road trip. The first summer in Savannah, we let Tina Dawn invite a friend from Macon to join us for a weekend at the beach. We were still enthralled with this barrier island. We loved the "old school" beach that was like a beach from the fifties. We would put our chairs close to the Desoto motel. It was an old stucco motel with a pool. Paul said it looked like it could have been in the movie "Godzilla." They let you order grilled burgers and buy beer and hang out at their pool, even if you weren't staying there. You just could not be bold enough to bring in a cooler. The best was when they had music on the weekend.

That particular weekend, we heard something we have not heard before or since, "Layla" being played on an accordion. Tina Dawn and her friend Ann were having a ball, until Ann got caught up on some old metal from the Georgia Core of Engineers' past project and split open her foot. Back then, we did not have Urgent Care and had to spend the evening in the Emergency Room getting her stitched up. I really hate it when you pick up a perfectly good child to take her on vacation and bring her home stitched up.

As if that wasn't enough, Tina Dawn invited another friend to family beach day. She was a lovely child who had a beautiful singing voice. She was very sweet and well mannered. Tina Dawn and her friend walked on the beach and kept pretty much to themselves, as prepubescent girls do.

Paul made himself at home with his Scurvy Medicine and a lounge chair. I had a snoot full of Scurvy Medicine and decided it was time to roam down the beach, without my flip flops of course. The sand was burning hot and I was doing some high-stepping, spilling a little "medicine" as I went. Lo and behold, there were Doris and Will (Paul's law school friend, Tina Dawn's swim teacher, "big nose, big dick," as Doris fondly calls him). Of course, I ran over and joined them and their buddies. They were enjoying something, I don't remember if it was weed or "nose candy" but whatever it was, I was easily tempted and joined in.

Well, time just flew and I realized that I needed to take my blistered feet back to Paul and, oh yes, the children. Well, needless to say, Paul was less than enthused when

I returned, as he said, "Oh by the way, don't you have softball practice this afternoon?"

"Oh, hell yes, let's go," I said as we rounded up the girls. We gathered up the kids and stuff and got in the car. I poured myself into the front seat and we took off.

Just as we got onto the highway to head back towards town, I began to feel a bit queasy. Right when we were getting into town, I said: "pull over." Thankfully, Paul was a quick study and pulled right over.

I fell out of the car and was puking my guts out into the bushes as I heard Paul tell Tina Dawn, "Don't worry, your mother may be an alcoholic, but it could be worse." Well, Hell, I was seeing double and did not make softball practice. Hope Tina Dawn had a good time with her sweet, talented friend because her friend never came to visit again. When we got home, I spent a lot of time talking on that "great white telephone to God," otherwise known as a toilet, and calling everyone that I knew on the real telephone. What an awesome day at the beach.

I had to make sure that Paul finally had an awesome day at the beach, too. Tina Dawn was otherwise occupied and we took off to Tybee. It was a glorious sunny day. We parked and took off to the beach. The waves were just right as we went in to swim. We cuddled in the water and got all lustful and sultry and decided to have a little "afternoon delight." Yes, right out there in the ocean. We were hard, hot, and bothered and all was blissful, but I was better at holding on to my bathing suit bottoms than Paul. Next thing I knew, his bottoms were swept away on a wave and there he was, naked in the ocean.

After I guffawed a little, I said that I would run across the dunes to the parking lot and would get the car and come pick up "His Nakedness." I got out of the water and would run a little ways, then stop and laugh hysterically. "Arrogant attorney is naked in the ocean." Then I would run a few feet and double over into laughter again.

I finally got the car and picked up the naked Paul. We rode into the village of Tybee to a little beach shop so I could buy the naked man a bathing suit. I went in and purchased one from the little Oriental store clerk. I took it out to the car; he did not like it and sent me back to exchange it. The clerk was very nice and found me a second choice. Well, lo and behold, he did not like that one either. She was a little perturbed that I came back in so quickly for another exchange. I explained, "Well, we were out in the ocean and my husband lost his bathing suit. He is out in the car naked."

"Well," she said, "naked man in car should not be so choosy!"

Sizzlin' Summer

----◆----

Now, Paul always says that he did not say this, but he said, "You have got to find a summertime job." I knew he was right. The tuition for Tina Dawn's school was steep and we seemed to be saying "CHARGE" a lot to old MasterCard. I contacted my "go to guy" at the county office and he came through for me. I was signed on to leave the classroom for the next year and join him at the Central Office on the "Dark Side" (that is what we lovingly say about teachers who go into Administration) as a consultant.

I would have been sad to depart from my Irregulars, but we were all dispersing. Tamara would remain, but she was only at Victory Street School a couple days a week. Vera and Larry patched things up and she was retreating to not Las Vegas but a mutual choice for both husband and wife: San Francisco, California. Doris was hired at a more upscale school in Savannah. The Colonel and Emma were moving to Virginia. Eva and her hubby were relocating back home in Mississippi.

I was also hired to work on a manual during the summer on how to set up a Behavior Disorders classroom.

And Odell and I both landed a job together teaching in the enrichment program. Ain't that a stitch!!!! I was given the job of teaching Introduction to Special Education at Armstrong College, as well.

Armstrong is one of the campuses of Georgia Southern University. It is located just a few miles from the squares of historic downtown Savannah. I had been there before to take a class or two. One day, while there, it began to snow a few flakes. That was a rarity for Savannah. I panicked and shoved my old rattletrap Datsun B210 into gear and ran right over one of those concrete thingies that mark your parking space. Damn, that sure is a rough how do you do. I did not think of it again. Much later, when the whole underside of the car was cracked and in need of repair, Paul kept asking if I had run over anything. "No." Then one day I remembered that day in the Armstrong College parking lot. Oh, yeah, that. I guess I did run over something.

Well anyway, I felt real privileged to be asked to teach a class there. That filled my summer right up until it was time to start my new administrative position. Paul, of course he does not remember this, was ecstatic. It was about this same time when Tina Dawn was to celebrate her birthday, and she always had to have a party.

It was sure easy to do the party invites. It was her whole class, with the girls spending the night. One of the girls' moms wanted to help, so she bought all the girls panties. Yes, panties. I found that odd, but they were cute panties. That evening, we showed them the movie, "West Side Story." They were so cute walking around doing that clicking sound and singing songs from the movie.

Now, shortly after the May 17th party, Paul found out via Mary Goldberg, our social worker friend from Cherryville, that there was a job opening at the Department of Social Services back home for a staff attorney. Paul jumped on the opportunity, using Mary as a reference. Well, lo and behold, he was hired and off he and Tina Dawn went to Cherryville. Hell yes, I said *off they went to C'ville.* They moved right in with my mom and dad. You might say, where in the hell was I? Well, hell, I was in Savannah doing those 3 summer jobs. I was so pissed that my contribution to packing was packing one plate that broke. Where was I going to live????

Emma and The Colonel had a beautiful condo with a pool out on the south side. They were going to be gone and offered it to me free of charge. They are the greatest. But did I go there? No. I went to live with Buck and Lois in what I will lovingly call a modest home. Hell, it was summer in Savannah and it had no air. I was sleeping on a mattress on the floor. We began an easy, sultry, sizzlin' summer lifestyle, until I began to feel very sick. I had a high fever and big, gigantic lymph nodes. And oh man, the white in my eyes was yellow and my face was, too. Guess it was time to go to the doctor.

He asked if I had been bitten by a tick, by any chance. Well, I had done some playing in the woods, so to speak, and Paul had pulled a big, fat, blood-sucking tick off my head. Well, there you have it. I was struck with tick fever and had to take this Tetracycline pill. It made me feel almost as sick as the fever. I told Odell if I fell out at work, just step over me and carry on.

You should have seen Odell and me. Instead of picking him up at home each morning, he had me cruise through a grocery store parking lot and slow down, then he jumped into the car. Not sure what that was all about. We had a ball with the enrichment kids. My class at Armstrong was great. I had eager students, and at the end of the session, they gave me a music box with a magic hat on top, in honor of The Magic Kids. I will always have a reminder of my Magic Kids at Victory Street School. I have it to this day.

During all this work and sickness, Doris came by Lois and Buck's one night and said I just had to come out with her to a bar. I said, "No, I feel like warmed-over hell." She offered me a tiny white pill that would make me ever so much better, but I declined. I did get my sick ass up and accompanied her to the bar.

There was a bouncer at the door and I said, "We are Doris and Annie and we come together." He let us right in and we sat close to the stage where the band was playing. The lead singer was cute and, right before the break, someone mentioned that it was his 21st birthday. During the break, we invited him right over to our table and ordered him a drink.

He and Doris were having a lively conversation when I noticed something white was floating in his drink. "Doris, did you slip the singer a mickey?" She just grinned as she was giving him her phone number. I said that it was time to go and we departed. I was not in the mood for that kind of crazy. She dropped me off at Lois and Buck's and I regaled them with the story of "slip a mickey" night and then went to bed.

The next day, I was invited to a pool party at the apartment complex where one of my softball girlfriends lived. I had just taken off my cover-up and was getting ready to approach my friends when I saw a large guy giving a commanding performance to the girls by the pool. He said that they would not believe what happened at the bar last night. These two chicks came in and slipped our lead singer a "mickey" during break, and when he returned to the stage, he passed out face down on the stage. I turned around and slithered away before he could see me and say "That's her!" That was a close call!

Paul came to visit. Lois, Buck, and I were sitting in the den with our feet in pans of water trying to get cool. He flipped out. "You crazies look like The Grapes of Wrath. Get up right now! We are all moving to the air-conditioned condo." We did and, of course, we had a nice, cool, restful weekend.

Sizzlin' summer ended and I drove myself home to North Carolina, ending my sojourn in Savannah. When I pulled up to my parents' home, there was a big yellow ribbon tied around the old oak tree, just like in the song "Tie a Yellow Ribbon Around the Old Tree" just for me.

The Victory Street Irregulars Reunite

---◆---

Victory Street Irregulars Reunion Rules, written by Tamara, Our Diva

Motto: Break Rules, Talk Trash, Laugh a Lot and Real Loud

Mission: Avoid Suspicion

Vision: Avoid Prison

Conviction: Avoid Eviction; don't get convicted!

Membership: Restricted to those suffering from PTTS Syndrome (Post Traumatic Teaching Stress Syndrome)

Initiation: Waived if you taught at Victory Street School. You have suffered enough.

Dues: Waived except for the occasional request for funds to cover emergencies such as bail, attorney fees, court costs, etc.

After our group all ventured away from Savannah, we managed to keep in touch. Our adventures and traumas together as educators and irregulars at Victory Street School certainly produced a special bond.

One summer, about five years after we departed from Victory Street School, Doris organized a reunion of sort because she was going to visit her brother in the North Carolina Blue Ridge Mountains at a resort called Holly Springs. Doris communicated with Tamara, Emma, Eva, and me about arrival days, sleep arrangements, and so forth. Unfortunately, Vera could not make the trip in from San Francisco.

Doris and I met early at Holly Springs and drove to Franklin, North Carolina for a meal out. We had an enjoyable dinner at an Italian restaurant and, of course, true to form, Doris turned on her vamping charms with the cute, young waiter. He came home with us to play.

I definitely have difficulty with a Northern girl's sense of romance, even when they are in the South. This was a hot summer and Doris just had to make a fire in the fireplace in our cabin. No, I do not mean her "personal fire" with the waiter but an oh-my-God, log-burning fire. It was so hot in there that I could not prance around since I had a sweat mustache and was *swussy* (that is, sweating at both ends). I thought all was well when I got up the next day for morning mimosas, but that was when Doris realized that the cute, young waiter had left his wallet. We got dressed right quick and went back to the Italian restaurant to return his wallet. We met up with the lady (I use that term loosely) restaurant owner who snatched up that wallet right out of Doris's pretty little hand and promptly threw us out of the restaurant and said that we were banned from ever returning to that restaurant. Who gets banned from a restaurant in Franklin, North Carolina?

We went back to Holly Springs to join the other Irregulars for a picnic out by the creek. It was a beautiful area with large rocks and a cool creek running through it. We were all proud of still having a little stun factor dressed in our bathing suits with Miss Mississippi Eva leading the way. Now, we were all mighty fine-looking women but hell, she was drop-dead gorgeous! We ate our picnic, which included North Carolina BBQ, and took pictures and talked all afternoon about our lives and pranks in Savannah and our current lives beyond. We were like lizards sunning on a rock. Then it was time to go back to our cabins and get gussied up for nighttime.

Emma and The Colonel had a van and we all piled in for The Colonel, our chauffeur, to drive us to dinner at a restaurant in Sky Valley. Doris's brother met us there. I always loved her brother. He was so damn cute and funny. Of course, the first thing I did was moon him from the top of the staircase as my form of hello, which had all the Irregulars screaming and carrying on about my irreverence in a nice restaurant. It was mine and Doris's brother's traditional greeting. As usual, he would comment on my cute ass, the *gold standard* as he called it. He always asked for a re-tell of my many funny stories. The Irregulars went on to get drinks from the bar.

It was then that we realized that we had a problem. The kitchen was closed for the night. Doris was talking about how we really wanted to eat there when The Chef came out. WOW!!!! We all made little audible gasps (well Doris's brother and The Colonel didn't). The Chef was a hunk of gorgeous man with a beautiful accent. Tamara, our Diva, verbalized the sentiment, "He's hot as a match." That Tamara was wild as always. I think he sensed the climate and said that he would go back to the kitchen and make us a special dish. Hell, he *was* a special dish. We were delighted and took our seats. The meal was a fabulous shrimp and pasta dish that we all enjoyed. And, you guessed it, Doris invited him to come back to the cabin with us.

I did say it was a van, but it was a little crowded. The Chef just climbed in and sat on the floor. We had a hilarious ride back with all of us laughing and talking at the same time.

We got back and disappeared into our cabins. Doris made a f...ing fire, of course. Doris and I put on a bikini fashion show for The Chef, which naturally included whipped cream.

Now, our Diva, Tamara was also staying in the same cabin. Her prior behavior in Savannah had worn off and she retired into her bedroom. No bikini fashion show or whipped cream for her. Well, I soon joined her and went to bed.

The next day, Doris drove The Chef back and Tamara said to me that we needed to have a little talk with our Doris.

When she returned, we tried to talk to her about her dangerous *chef behavior* over the last couple of days.

But Holy Cow, she was in love with The Chef! They had plans to continue to get to know one another.

Well, the good news is that they did indeed marry each other, and this was only the beginning of wonderful reunions and a forever friendship between the Victory Street Irregulars.

Epilogue 2020

———◆———

Who Found *The Love of Their Life*?

Everyone.

Annie. Still in love with the picky bathing-suit selector. Still saying that she is going to retire so she can spend more time with her wonderful grandchild and the rowdy Irregulars. She celebrated the *End of The Eighties* by always knowing who the designated driver was.

Doris. Totally, completely committed to The Chef, their successful gourmet restaurant, and her three absolutely delightful adult children. She organized another banging reunion when her daughter married in 2019. She is still working as a dedicated educator and Reading Specialist.

Emma. The Colonel did reform his zipper problem, although some super-nagging from the Irregulars did take place. They have two amazing, brilliant adult daughters. After following The Colonel around the country, the lovely Emma finally got to settle in beautiful Maryland. The Irregulars revere The Colonel for navigating the lovely Emma through some difficult illnesses, which, by the way, were not related to her earlier shin injuries.

Eva. Everything about her wedding was gorgeous. Except for the uninvited guest; you may have figured it out: Mississippi, summer 1985. Yes, Hurricane Elena. The reception was cut a bit short. Eva and her three incredibly accomplished adult children miss their beloved Cary, who tragically died way too early of a heart attack. Eva retired in 2009 and travels around the world with her many friends, including Tamara. Lunches are now always welcome.

Tamara. Our Diva found the Love of Her Life and invited us all to their wedding, and because we were SO HAPPY for her, we followed all of her rules! Our talking, dancing, and laughing were loud and crazy, but there was no suspicious activity. The Irregulars later supported Tamara through a terrible time when her charming sweetheart went through, and succumbed to, that damn cancer, far too soon in their fairy-tale relationship.

Vera. Returned to Statman, and they to Berkeley, where she earned her doctorate in education. They have two adult children and *three most adorable and perceptive* grandchildren. Statman soon discovered online Fantasy Sports, about the same thrill as poker, but their year apart cemented their commitment to each other. They revel in retirement.

The Irregulars have managed to have five reunions and are thirsty for more. Please buy more copies of this book so they can afford to.

Meet the Author

———◆———

Sadie Allran Broome has been a public-school educator, teaching students with disabilities, for over forty years. During that time, she has been "Teacher of the Year" in Gaston County, North Carolina and Bibb County, Georgia. She co-authored three books on teaching character in the elementary, middle, and teenage years. She was a Christa McAuliffe Fellow and Non-Teaching Educator of the Year in Gaston County Schools. Her works have been published in two journals and she recently collaborated with an educator in the United Kingdom on a research article. Sadie was a recipient of the Cardinal Award and the Order of the Long Leaf Pine Award in the state of North Carolina.

Sadie is at home in Cherryville, North Carolina. She is married to Dennis and is a proud mother and grandmother.

Made in the USA
Columbia, SC
19 November 2020